CERTIFICATION CIRCLE™

MOUS

D1317582

Microsoft PowerPoint 2002

Rachel Bunin

COMPREHENSIVE

APPROVED COURSEWARE

COURSE
TECHNOLOGY

THOMSON LEARNING

Australia • Canada • Mexico • Singapore • Spain • United Kingdom • United States

MOUS Microsoft PowerPoint 2002

CERTIFICATION CIRCLE™ COMPREHENSIVE
Rachel Bunin

Managing Editor:
Nicole Jones Pinard

Product Managers:
Debbie Masi
Julia Healy

Editorial Assistant:
Christina Kling Garrett

Production Editor:
Debbie Masi

Contributing Author:
Carol Cram

Developmental Editors:
Marjorie Hunt, Kim Crowley

Composition House:
GEX Publishing Services

QA Manuscript Reviewers:
Nicole Ashton, John Freitas,
Jeff Schwartz, Alex White

Book Designers:
Joseph Lee, black fish design

ISBN 0-619-05672-X

Printed in Canada

1 2 3 4 5 6 7 8 9 WC 06 05 04 03 02

For more information, contact Course Technology, 25 Thomson Place, Boston, Massachusetts, 02210.

Or you can visit us on the World Wide Web at www.course.com

Thank You, Advisory Board!

This book is a result of the hard work and dedication by authors, editors, and more than 30 instructors focused on Microsoft Office and MOUS certification. These instructors formed our Certification Circle Advisory Board. We looked to them to flesh out our original vision and turn it into a sound pedagogical method of instruction. In short, we asked them to partner with us to create *the* book for preparing for a MOUS Exam. And, now we wish to thank them for their contributions and expertise.

ADVISORY BOARD MEMBERS:

Linda Amergo	Old Westbury
Shellie Besharse	Mississippi County Community College
Margaret Britt	Copiah Lincoln Community College
Becky Burt	Copiah Lincoln Community College
Judy Cameron	Spokane Community College
Elizabeth T. De Arazoza	Miami-Dade Community College
Susan Dozier	Tidewater Community College
Dawna Dewire	Babson College
Pat Evans	J. Sargent Reynolds
Susan Fry	Boise State University
Joyce Gordon	Babson College
Steve Gordon	Babson College
Pat Harley	Howard Community College
Rosanna Hartley	Western Piedmont Community College
Eva Hefner	St. Petersburg Junior College
Becky Jones	Richland College
Mali Jones	Johnson and Wales University
Angie McCutcheon	Washington State Community College
Barbara Miller	Indiana University
Carol Milliken	Kellogg Community College
Maureen Paparella	Monmouth University
Mike Puopolo	Bunker Hill Community College
Kathy Proittel	Essex Community College
Pamela M. Randall	Unicity Network
Theresa Savarese	San Diego City College
Barbara Sherman	Buffalo State
Kathryn Surles	Salem Community College
Beth Thomas	Hagerstown Community College
Barbara Webber	Northern Essex Community College
Jean Welsh	Lansing Community College
Lynn Wermers	North Shore Community College
Sherry Young	Kingwood College

Preface

Welcome to the *CERTIFICATION CIRCLE SERIES*. Each book in this series is designed with one thing in mind: preparing you to pass a Microsoft Office User Specialist (MOUS) exam. This strict focus allows you to target the skills you need to be successful. You will not need to study anything extra—it's like getting a peek at the exam before you take it! Read on to learn more about how the book is organized and how you will get the most out of it.

Table of Contents

This book is organized around the MOUS exam objectives. Each Skill on the exam is taught on two facing pages with text on the left and figures on the right. This also makes for a terrific reference; if you want to brush up on a few skills, it's easy to find the ones you're looking for.

Getting Started Chapter

Each book begins with a Getting Started Chapter. This Chapter contains skills that are *not* covered on the exam but the authors felt were vital to understanding the software. The content in this chapter varies from application to application.

Skill Overview

Each skill starts with a paragraph explaining the concept and how you would use it. These are clearly written and concise.

File Open Icon

We provide a realistic project file for every skill. And, it's in the form you need it in order to work through the steps; there's no wasted time building the file before you can work with it.

Skill Steps

The Steps required to perform the skill appear on the left page with what you type in green text.

Tips

We provide tips specific to the skill or how the skill is tested on the exam.

Skill Set 8

Integrating with Other Applications

Import Data to Access
Import Data from an Excel Workbook

You can import data into an Access database from several file formats, including an Excel workbook or another Access, FoxPro, dBase, or Paradox database. It is not uncommon for a user to enter a list of data into Excel and later decide to convert that data into an Access database, because the user wants to use Access's extensive form or report capabilities or wants multiple people to be able to use the data at the same time. (An Access database is inherently **multi-user**; many people can enter and update data at the same time.) Since the data in an Excel workbook is structured similarly to data in an Access table datasheet, you can easily import data from an Excel workbook into an Access database by using the **Import Spreadsheet Wizard**.

Activity Steps

file Classes01.mdb

1. Click **File** on the menu bar, point to **Get External Data**, then click **Import**

2. Navigate to the drive and folder where your Project Files are stored, click the **Files of type list arrow**, click **Microsoft Excel**, click **Instructors**, then click **Import** to start the Import Spreadsheet Wizard
   See Figure 8-1.

3. Select the **First Row Contains Column Headings** check box, then click **Next**

4. Click **Next** to indicate that you want to create a new table, then click **Next** to not specify field changes

5. Click the **Choose my own primary key option button** to set InstructorID as the primary key field, then click **Next**

6. Type **Instructors** in the Import to Table box, click **Finish**, then click **OK**

7. Double-click **Instructors** to open it in Datasheet View
   See Figure 8-2. Imported data works the same way as any other table of data in a database.

8. Close the Instructors table

tip

Step 4
You can also import Excel workbook data into an existing table if the field names used in the Excel workbook match the field names in the Access table.

Additional Projects

For those who want more practice applying the skills they've learned, there is a project for each skill set located at the back of each book. The projects ask you to combine the skills you've learned to create a meaningful document – just what you do in real life.

Project for Skill Set 1

Working with Cells and Cell Data

Sales Projection for Alaska Adventures

You work for Alaska Adventures, a small company based in Juneau, Alaska, that offers sea kayaking, mountain biking, and hiking tours. You've received a workbook containing a sales projection for the sea kayaking tours that the company hopes to sell in the busy summer months of June, July, and August. In this project, you will complete and format this worksheet. The workbook also contains a second worksheet that includes a list of the guests who purchased sea kayaking tours on a single day during the previous summer. You'll use the AutoFilter features on this list to determine the number of customers who came from countries other then the United States and Canada.

Activity Steps

open EC_Project1.xls

1. Clear the contents and formats of cell A3, drag cell A4 up to cell A3, then delete cell D14 and shift the cells left
2. Merge cell A3 across cells A3 to E3, then check the spelling in the worksheet and correct any errors
3. Enter Total in cell C13, use the Go To command to navigate to cell C13, then change the value in cell C13 to 1200
4. Use the SUM function in cell E12 to add the values in cells B12 through D12, then copy the formula to cells E13 through E15

Step 8
To save time, press and hold the [CTRL] key, select each group of cells, and then click the Currency Style button.

5. Select cells B12 through B16, then use the AutoSum button to calculate the totals required for cells B16 through E16
6. In cell B18, enter the formula required to subtract the value in cell B16 from the value in cell B9, then copy the formula to cells C18 through E18
7. Use Find and Replace to locate all instances of 1500 and replace them with 500
8. Format cells B7 through E7, B9 through E9, B12 through E12, B16 through E16, and B18 through E18 with the Currency style, format cells B8 through E8 and cells B13 through E15 with the Comma style, then compare the completed worksheet to Figure EP 1-1
9. Switch to the Customers worksheet, then use AutoFilter to show only the International customers in the Category column. The filtered list appears as shown in Figure EP 1-2

close EC_Project1.xls

Skill 1
Import Data to Access

Figure 8-1: Import Spreadsheet Wizard dialog box

Figure 8-2: Imported Instructors table in Datasheet View

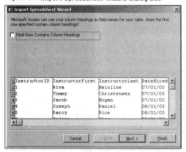

Seven records were imported

extra!

Using delimited text files

You can import data from a **delimited text file**, a file of unformatted data where each field value is delimited (separated) by a common character, such as a comma or a tab. Each record is further delimited by a common character, such as a paragraph mark. A delimited text file usually has a **txt** (for text) file extension. You can use delimited text files to convert data from a proprietary software system (such as an accounting, inventory, or scheduling software system) into a format that other programs can import. For example, most accounting software programs won't export data directly into an Access database, but they can export data to a delimited text file, which can then be imported by Access.

Figures

There are at least two figures per skill which serve as a reference as you are working through the steps. Callouts focus your attention to what's important.

Extra Boxes

This will *not* be on the exam–it's extra–hence the name. But, there are some very cool things you can do with Office xp so we had to put this stuff somewhere!

Target Your Skills

At the end of each unit, there are two Target Your Skills exercises. These require you to create a document from scratch, based on the figure, using the skills you've learned in the chapter. And, the solution is provided– there's no wasted time trying to figure out if you've done it right.

Additional Resources

There are many resources available with this book—both free and for a nominal fee. Please see your sales representative for more information. The resources available with this book are:

INSTRUCTOR'S MANUAL

Available as an electronic file, the Instructor's Manual is quality-assurance tested and includes unit overviews, lecture topics, solutions to all lessons and projects, and extra Target Your Skills. The Instructor's Manual is available on the Instructor's Resource Kit CD-ROM, or you can download if from www.course.com.

FACULTY ONLINE COMPANION

You can browse this textbook's password protected site to obtain the Instructor's Manual, Solution Files, Project Files, and any updates to the text. Contact your Customer Service Representative for the site address and password.

PROJECT FILES

Project Files contain all of the data that students will use to complete the lessons and projects. A Readme file includes instructions for using the files. Adopters of this text are granted the right to install the Project Files on any stand-alone computer or network. The Project Files are available on the Instructor's Resource Kit CD-ROM, the Review Pack, and can also be downloaded from www.course.com.

SOLUTION FILES

Solution Files contain every file students are asked to create or modify in the lessons and projects. A Help file on the Instructor's Resource Kit includes information for using the Solution Files.

FIGURE FILES

Figure Files contain all the figures from the book in bitmap format. Use the figure files to create transparency masters or in a PowerPoint presentation.

SAM, SKILLS ASSESSMENT MANAGER FOR MICROSOFT OFFICE XP SAM^{xp}

SAM is the most powerful Office XP assessment and reporting tool that will help you gain a true understanding of your students' proficiency in Microsoft Word, Excel, Access, and PowerPoint 2002.

TOM, TRAINING ONLINE MANAGER FOR MICROSOFT OFFICE XP TOM

TOM is Course Technology's MOUS-approved training tool for Microsoft Office XP. Available via the World Wide Web and CD-ROM, TOM allows students to actively learn Office XP concepts and skills by delivering realistic practice through both guided and self-directed simulated instruction.

Certification Circle Series, SAM, and TOM: the true training and assessment solution for Office XP.

Contents

MOUS Microsoft PowerPoint 2002

CERTIFICATION CIRCLE™ *COMPREHENSIVE*

Skill List

1. Start PowerPoint
2. Understand PowerPoint views
3. Work with objects
4. Get Help
5. Save files

PowerPoint 2002 is the presentation graphics program that is part of Microsoft Office XP. You can use PowerPoint to create presentation materials, including computer-based slide shows, 35 mm slides, transparencies, handouts, and speaker notes. Using PowerPoint, you can create professional-looking presentations to teach concepts, advertise products, entertain an audience, or simply convey a message. Slides can contain static or animated text and graphics as well as video to help express your ideas. In this skill set, you will learn how to start and exit the program, open, save, and close files. You will learn the elements that comprise the PowerPoint window, many of which will look familiar to you if you have worked with other Microsoft Office applications. PowerPoint has several different views that you use for different purposes. You will learn how to switch among views and understand the type of work you can do in each one. You will also learn how to get help using the extensive PowerPoint Help system.

Getting Started

Getting Started with PowerPoint 2002

Start PowerPoint
Start and Exit PowerPoint

There are many ways to start PowerPoint. The way you choose will depend on your personal working style as well as the task at hand. You can click the Start button on the taskbar and then click PowerPoint from the Programs menu. You can also double-click the PowerPoint icon on the desktop if one was created. You can click the New Office Document command on the Start Menu to open the New Office Document dialog box and then click the Presentations tab to start a new presentation from the available templates. You also have several options for exiting the program, including the Close button on the title bar and the Exit command on the File menu.

Step 3
To exit PowerPoint, you can also click File on the menu bar, then click Exit.

Activity Steps

1. Click the **Start button** on the taskbar, then point to **Programs**
   See Figure GS-1.

2. Click **Microsoft PowerPoint** on the Programs menu
   PowerPoint opens, with a blank presentation open.
   See Figure GS-2.

3. Click the **Close button** on the title bar to exit the program

Figure GS-1: Programs menu

Click to open New Office Document dialog box

Desktop icons will differ on your computer

Programs

Click to start PowerPoint

The Start button

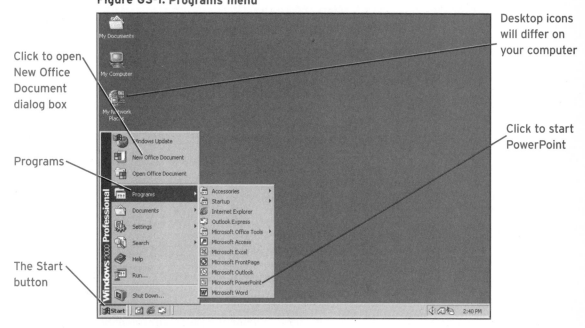

Figure GS-2: The PowerPoint window

File menu

Click to exit program

Click to close current presentation

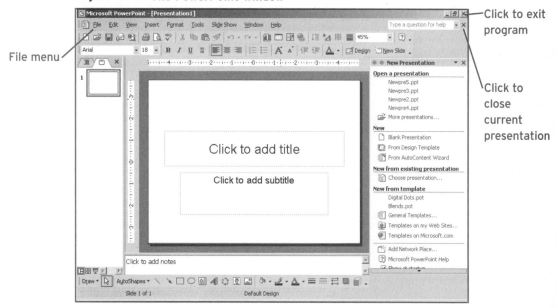

Getting Started

Getting Started with PowerPoint 2002

Understand PowerPoint Views
View the PowerPoint Window

Like other Office applications, PowerPoint has **menus** and **toolbars** from which you choose commands to perform actions. PowerPoint also has a **task pane**, which is a window that opens on the right side of your screen and gives you access to many commonly used commands. The task pane changes depending on what action you are performing. You can change task panes by clicking the Other Task panes arrow, or close the task pane if you want more room to work on the slide in the window. When you first open PowerPoint, a blank presentation opens in the **presentation window**.

Activity Steps

If your computer is not set up to show file extensions, you won't see ppt in the title bar after the filename. To change this setting, open the Control Panel in Windows, double-click Folder Options, click the View tab, then remove the check box from Hide file extensions for known file types.

1. **Start PowerPoint to open a blank presentation, then point to the title bar**
   The **title bar** has the Program name as well as the current filename on the left. Because this is a blank presentation, it has the temporary filename Presentation1. *See Figure GS-3.*

2. **Point to File on the menu bar**
   The **menu bar** includes the menus for accessing the PowerPoint commands. Click a menu name on the menu bar to open it and view the most commonly used menu commands. Double-click the menu item to view all the commands on that menu. The menu bar also has a **Close button** to close the presentation window and the **Ask a Question box** to get help.

3. **Point to but do not click the Open button ▣ on the Standard toolbar**
   A **ScreenTip**, a yellow box with the button name, appears to identify the command for each button. By default, the Standard and Formatting toolbars appear on two rows. You click a toolbar button to select the command.

4. **Point to the presentation window**
   The **presentation window** contains four work areas: the Slides tab, Outline tab, Slide pane, and Notes pane. The **ruler** helps you place objects on the slide.

5. **Point to the View buttons**
   The View buttons change the way you view your presentation; Normal (for working on individual slides), Slide Sorter (for arranging slide order), and Slide Show (for viewing your presentation as a slide show).

6. **Point to the Status bar**
   The **Status bar** displays several indicators to help you as you work, such as the title of the slide you are viewing and the total number of slides in the presentation.

Figure GS-3: Elements in the PowerPoint window

Title bar
Menu bar
Standard toolbar
Outline tab
Slides tab
Notes pane
View buttons
Drawing toolbar

Minimize, Restore, Close buttons
Formatting toolbar
New Presentation task pane
Ruler
Slide pane
Status bar

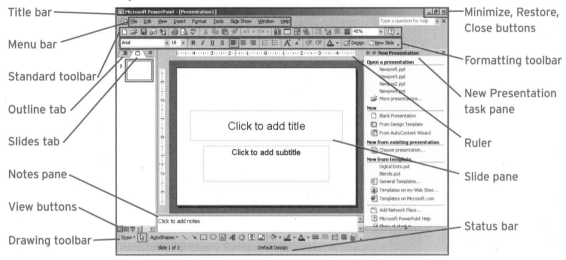

extra!

Minimizing, maximizing, and restoring Windows

On the far right end of the title bar are three control buttons for controlling the PowerPoint program window: the **Minimize button**, the **Restore button**, and the **Close button**. Minimized windows appear as buttons on the taskbar. If you click the Minimize button on the PowerPoint window title bar, the PowerPoint window will minimize and become a button on the taskbar. You can restore the window by clicking that taskbar button. If you click the Maximize button for any window, it will display as a full screen. If you click the Restore button on a window that you just maximized, the window will be restored to its previous size. You can also double-click the title bar of a window to maximize it or restore it to its previous size. To minimize all open windows, you can click the Show desktop button on the Quick Launch bar (if it is active) on the taskbar. To close a window, click the Close button on the taskbar. To close a window that has been minimized, you can right-click the taskbar button, then click Close.

Getting Started

Getting Started with PowerPoint 2002

Understand PowerPoint Views
Open and Close a Presentation

There are many ways to open a PowerPoint file, or **presentation**. Once again, the way you choose will depend on your personal working style and the task at hand. If you want to start with a blank presentation, you can just start PowerPoint from the Programs menu. If you have an existing file you want to open and continue working on, you can use the New Presentation task pane to open a file using the Open dialog box. If you are done with a specific file but want to keep PowerPoint open so you can work on another, you can close the file by using the Close command on the File menu.

NOTE: Understanding the file icons: In this activity you learn how to open a file. Most of the other activities in this book require that you open a file at the beginning of the steps in order to complete the steps for that activity. When an activity requires that you open a file to complete the steps, you will see ⬛ above Step 1 with the filename of the file you need to open. ⬛ will appear at the end of the steps to remind you to close the file. Unless your instructor tells you to do otherwise, you should close the file without saving your changes.

Before you begin to work though the activities in this book, it is recommended that you make a backup copy of all the Project Files that are supplied with this book and store them in a safe place.

Activity Steps

Step 2
You can also open the Open dialog box by clicking File on the menu bar, then clicking Open or by clicking the Open button on the toolbar.

1. If the New Presentation task pane is not open, click **File** on the menu bar, then click **New** to open it

2. Click **More presentations** in the Open a presentation section of the task pane to open the Open dialog box
   See Figure GS-4.

3. Click the **Look in list arrow**, locate your Project Files, click **Newpre1.ppt**, then click the **Open list arrow**
   This menu gives you options for opening a file in special ways. Open as Read-Only protects the file from being overwritten. Open as Copy opens a copy of the file that you can rename so that the original file remains intact.

4. Click **Open**
   The Newpre1.ppt presentation file opens in the PowerPoint window. *See Figure GS-5.*

5. Click **File** on the menu bar, then click **Close**
   The presentation closes but PowerPoint is still running.

Figure GS-4: The Open dialog box

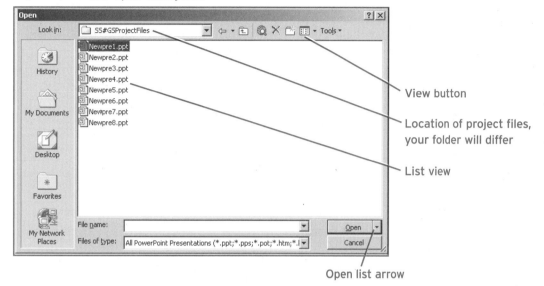

View button

Location of project files, your folder will differ

List view

Open list arrow

Figure GS-5: Presentation open in the PowerPoint window

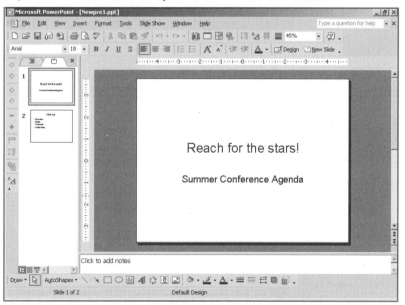

extra!

Changing views in the Open dialog box

The Open dialog box can display files in eight different views. Click the Views list arrow to select from Large Icons, Small Icons, List, Details, Properties, Preview, and Thumbnail views. Select Preview to see the first slide in a small preview window to help you locate the file you need.

Getting Started

Getting Started with PowerPoint 2002

Understand PowerPoint Views
Use Toolbars, Menus, and the Task Pane

Working on a presentation requires that you access the many commands available in PowerPoint to place, format, create, edit, and work with objects and slides. Commands are available through the menu bar, various toolbars, task panes, dialog boxes, and short-cut menus.

This activity requires that you open the file Newpre2.ppt. You can use the More presentations command on the task pane to locate and open this file.

Step 1

As you work, PowerPoint places the commands that you have used most recently on the short menu that displays when you click a menu name. To display all available commands on a menu, double-click the menu name or click the arrows at the bottom of the short menu. If you wait a few seconds, a short menu will automatically expand to the complete menu.

Activity Steps

 open Newpre2.ppt

1. Double-click **View** on the menu bar

2. Click **Task Pane**
   The New Presentation task pane opens. *See Figure GS-6.*

3. Click the **Other Task Panes list arrow** in the New Presentation task pane
   A list of the task panes available in PowerPoint opens. To open a specific task pane, click its name on the list.

4. Click **View** on the menu bar, notice that Task Pane has a shaded box with a check mark in it to indicate that it is open, then click **Task Pane** to close the task pane
   You can also close the task pane by clicking its Close button.

5. Double-click **Reach** on the slide, then click the **Bold button** B
   By default, the Formatting toolbar is located below the Standard toolbar and contains buttons for enhancing the appearance of your presentation. Some toolbars are **floating** and open when you need them. You can move toolbars to get them out of your way or you can **dock** toolbars to place them in a specific spot; the next time they open they will appear in that place. You can drag a toolbar to a new location, even after it is docked.

6. Click **Format** on the menu bar, then click **Font**
   The Font dialog box opens. You use dialog boxes to choose options for completing a particular task.

7. Click **Regular** in the Font style box to remove the bold, click **OK** to close the dialog box, then right-click **Reach**
   The shortcut menu has many commands that you might use at this time.

8. Right-click any toolbar
   See Figure G-7. Toolbars can be opened at any time by right-clicking the toolbar, then selecting the toolbar you need.

9. Press [Esc] to close the toolbar menu

 close Newpre2.ppt

Figure GS-6: Accessing commands

View menu

Open button

Format menu

New Presentation task pane

If the file you want to open is listed here, click the link

Click to close task pane

Other Task Panes list arrow

Click to open a new blank presentation

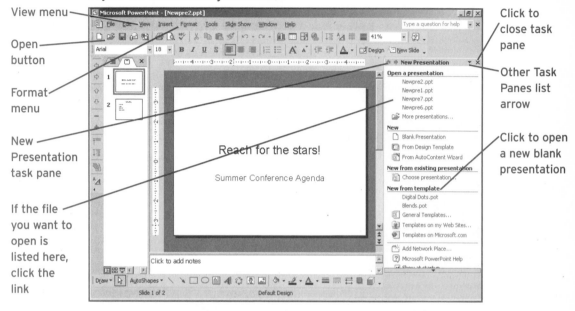

Figure GS-7: Viewing open toolbars

Bold button

Outlining toolbar is docked here

Drawing toolbar is docked here

Open toolbars have check marks

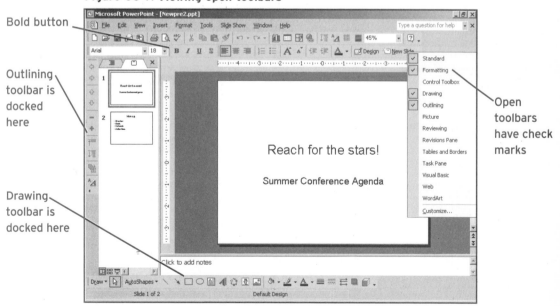

Getting Started

Getting Started with PowerPoint 2002

Understand PowerPoint Views
Change Views

PowerPoint has three views that you can use to create and modify presentations: The default view is **Normal view**, which you use to create and modify individual slides. Normal view has four work areas: the **Outline tab**, where you can work with the text on slides, the **Slides tab**, where you navigate among all your slides and get an overview of the entire presentation, the **Slide pane**, where you work with both text and graphic elements on an individual slide, and the **Notes pane** (located below the Slide pane), where you can enter speaker notes. You use **Slide Sorter view** for arranging the order of your slides, creating animation and transition effects (which you will learn about later), and for getting a bird's eye view of every slide in your presentation at once. You use Slide Show view to view the slides as a slide show. In Slide Show view, each slide fills the full screen. You can change from one view to another by clicking the View buttons, or using the commands on the View menu.

Activity Steps

 open Newpre3.ppt

You can choose whether to view your slides in color, grayscale, or black and white. Click View on the menu bar, point to Color/Grayscale, then click either Color, Grayscale, or Pure Black and White.

1. **Double-click View on the menu bar to see all the view commands**
   See Figure GS-8. Normal is selected, indicating that you are in Normal view.

2. **Click outside the menu to close it, then click the Outline tab**
   The Outline tab displays the text on each slide in outline formatting.

3. **Click the Slides tab**
   The Slides tab shows thumbnails of the slides.

4. **Click Slide 2 on the Slides tab, then click Slide 1**
   You can move quickly to a specific slide by clicking it on the Slides tab or Outline tab.

5. **Click the Slide Sorter View button** 🔳
   See Figure GS-9.

6. **Click the Slide Show (from current slide) button** 🖥
   The slide show appears full screen on your computer.

7. **Press the [Spacebar] three times to view both slides and return to Normal view**

 close Newpre3.ppt

Figure GS-8: Normal view

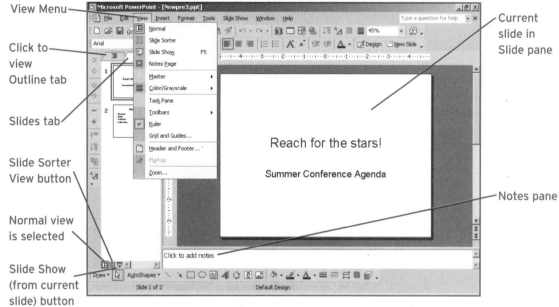

View Menu

Click to view Outline tab

Slides tab

Slide Sorter View button

Normal view is selected

Slide Show (from current slide) button

Current slide in Slide pane

Notes pane

Figure GS-9: Slide Sorter view

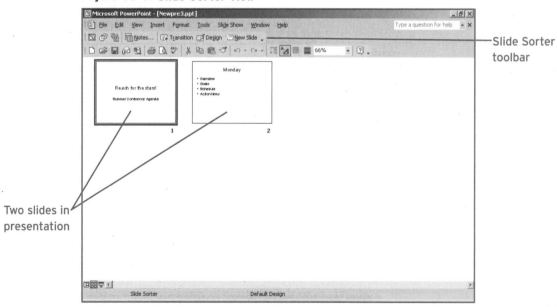

Slide Sorter toolbar

Two slides in presentation

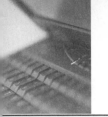

Getting Started

Getting Started with PowerPoint 2002

Understand PowerPoint Views
Work in Normal View

Depending on your work style and the task you are completing, you might find it helpful to rearrange parts of the Normal view window. For instance, if you want to see more of the slide on the screen but still want to use the Outline tab and Slides tab, you can reduce the width of the tabs by dragging the split bar. If you want to add a significant number of notes to the Notes pane, you could increase its height by dragging the split bar up. You can also close the Slides and Outline tabs by clicking the Close button on either tab. You can also move or resize the task pane as necessary to facilitate your work, or Zoom in and out to get a better view of your slides.

Step 2
To move the task pane to another location, drag its title bar.

Activity Steps

 open Newpre4.ppt

1. If the Ruler does not appear in the Normal view window, click **View** on the menu bar, then click **Ruler**

2. Place the pointer on the bar between the Slides tab and the vertical ruler so that the pointer changes to ←‖→, then drag ←‖→ to the left ¹/₂ " so that the thumbnails turn into icons

3. Place the pointer on the bar between the Slides tab and the vertical ruler, press and hold the left mouse button, drag ←‖→ to the right of the vertical ruler, release the mouse button, place the pointer on the bar between the Notes pane and the Slide pane, then drag ⇕ up to the 2" mark on the vertical ruler
   See Figure GS-10.

4. Click the **Close button** on the Slides tab
   Both the Slides tab and Notes pane close, giving you more room to work in the Slide pane.

5. Click **View** on the menu bar, then click **Normal (Restore Panes)**

6. Double-click **View** on the menu bar, then click **Zoom**
   See Figure G-11. You can change the Zoom percentage to see more or less detail on any slide by opening the Zoom dialog box or by clicking the Zoom list arrow on the toolbar.

7. Click **Cancel**

 close Newpre4.ppt

Figure GS-10: Changing the size of the panes

Zoom list arrow

Close button

Vertical ruler

Notes pane resized

Drag split bars to resize panes

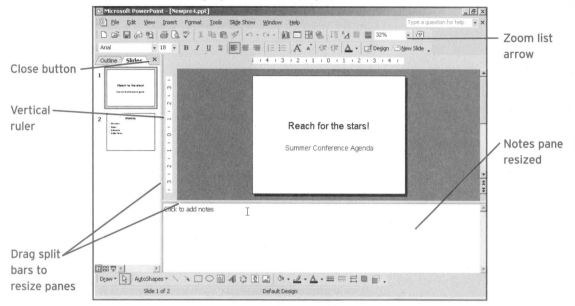

Figure GS-11: Zoom dialog box

Getting Started

Work with Objects
Select and Move Objects

When you create a presentation, your slides will probably contain a combination of text and graphics. In PowerPoint, all graphics are objects that you can move or resize. All text is stored in **placeholders** or textboxes, which are also objects that you can move and resize. To move, resize, or make formatting changes to an object, you first have to select it. How you select an object determines whether you are working with the object or the contents of the object. To select a text placeholder so that you can edit or format the text contained in it, click in the placeholder so that the insertion point changes to an I-beam. To move or resize a placeholder, click in the placeholder to select it, then click its border so that the edge changes to a dot pattern.

tip

To select more than one object at a time, select an object, press and hold [Shift], then click another object.

Activity Steps

 open Newpre5.ppt

1. Click **Slide 2** on the Slides tab, then click **Overview**
   Round **sizing handles** appear on the edges of the left text placeholder, indicating that it is selected. The border of slanted lines indicates that you can edit, enter, or format the text now. The I-beam pointer will place the insertion point wherever you click. The blinking vertical line is the insertion point, where any keyboard action you complete will appear. *See Figure GS-12.*

2. Double-click **items** to select this word
   Text selecting and editing in PowerPoint is similar to how you might edit a document file in a word processor such as Microsoft Word.

3. Click the **placeholder border**
   The border is now a dotted border.

4. Place the pointer on the border so that the pointer changes to ⁺↖, then drag down slightly
   See Figure GS-13.

5. Click outside the object to deselect it, press [Tab] to select the **Monday** text placeholder, then press [Tab] three times to cycle through all the objects on the slide and to select the clip art
   The clip art is selected. Sizing handles surround the image, and a green rotation handle is at the top.

6. Press [Esc] to deselect the object and close the Picture toolbar

 close Newpre5.ppt

Figure GS-12: Object selected for editing

Sizing handles

I beam pointer for editing, click to place insertion point in text

Diagonal border

Text placeholder object selected for editing

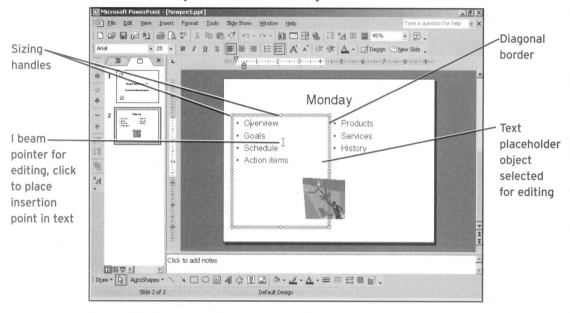

Figure GS-13: Moving or formatting an object

Move pointer

Dashed line shows new position of object

Object selected for formatting or moving

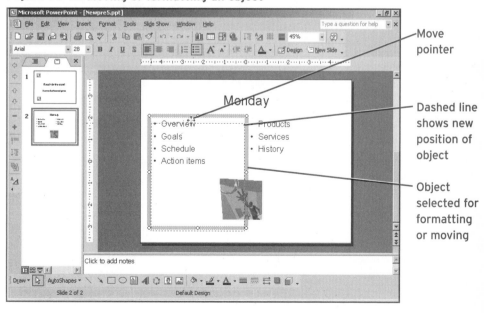

Getting Started

Getting Started with PowerPoint 2002

Get Help
Use the Help System

PowerPoint has a very impressive collection of features and tools. To take advantage of all it has to offer to create the best presentations possible, you will sometimes need help. The extensive Help system provided with PowerPoint is easy to access and can provide you with answers to your questions or give steps on how to complete tasks. You can access the Help system by typing a question in the Ask a Question box. You can search contents just as you would a table of contents in a book. You can also find out what specific items are on the screen by clicking Help on the menu bar, clicking What's This?, and then pointing to an item to get an explanation. Help is always available by pressing F1, which opens the Office Assistant. Help is available whether you are working on a presentation or you just have PowerPoint open.

Activity Steps

1. Click Type a question for help in the Ask a Question box on the menu bar, type How do I create a presentation?, press [Enter], then click About creating presentations
See Figure GS-14.

2. Click Show All
All blue linked text is expanded to show green definitions.

3. Click the Index tab if necessary, type view in the Type keywords box, then click Search to see a list of topics

4. Click the Contents tab, click the Expand button [+] to the left of Microsoft PowerPoint Help, click the Expand button [+] to the left of Getting Started, click What's installed with Microsoft PowerPoint 2002, then click Show All

5. Click the Answer Wizard tab, type Get Help, press [Enter], then click Show All
See Figure GS-15.

6. Click the Help window Close button

If the Tabs window is not open, click the Show button on the Help Window toolbar.

Figure GS-14: The Help window

Type keyword for search then click Search

Topics will appear here

Click to display all content on page

Scroll to see more

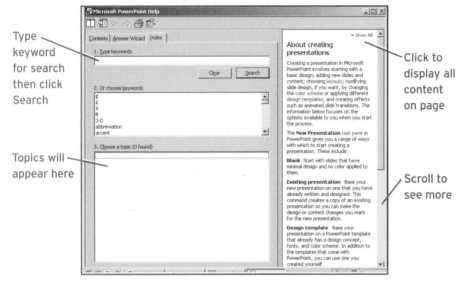

Figure GS-15: Results of get help search

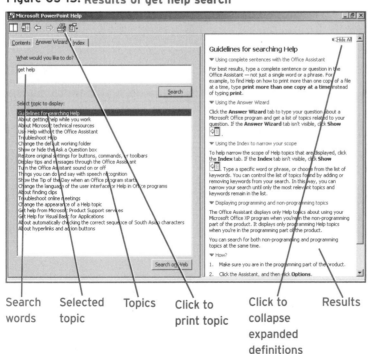

Search words

Selected topic

Topics

Click to print topic

Click to collapse expanded definitions

Results

Getting Started

Getting Started with PowerPoint 2002

Save Files
Save a Presentation

After you work long and hard on your presentation, you want to be sure to save it in a secure place. When you save a file, you copy the version of the file that is currently in the computer's memory onto storage media. This could be a hard disk or a floppy disk. There are many different ways to save files. To save a file for the first time, you click the Save button on the Standard toolbar to open the Save As dialog box. You use this dialog box to give the file a filename and specify the folder where you want to save it. **Filenames** are names used to identify files on storage media. If you have been working on a presentation that was saved previously and decide that you want to save an updated version of it while retaining the original file, you can use the Save As command to save it with a new name. If you know before you begin to create your presentation that you want to base a new presentation on an existing one, you can use the Choose presentation command on the New Presentation task pane. This command lets you open a copy of an existing presentation and save it with a new filename. If you click the Save button after working on a file that was previously saved, the file will be saved using the current filename, and the existing file will be overwritten with the changes you made.

Activity Steps

 open Newpre6.ppt

1. Click **File** on the menu bar, then click **Save As**
   The Save As dialog box opens as shown in Figure GS-16.

2. To rename the file, click to the right of the 6 in the File name box, type **-new**, then click **Save**

PowerPoint presentation files have a .ppt file extension that is added to all saved presentation files by default.

3. Double-click **stars!**, click the **Bold button** B on the toolbar, then click the **Save button** on the toolbar
   The change is saved in the Newpre6-new presentation.

4. Click **View** on the menu bar, click **Task Pane**, click the **Other Task Panes list arrow**, click **New Presentation**, then click **Choose presentation** in the New from existing presentation section
   The New from Existing Presentation dialog box opens.
   See Figure GS-17.

5. Click **Newpre6.ppt**, then click **Create New**
   The presentation opens with the default name Presentation2.

6. Click the **Save button** to open the Save As dialog box

7. Click **Save** to save the file with the name **Reach for the stars!.ppt**

 close Reach for the Stars!.ppt
   close Newpre6-new.ppt

Figure GS-16: Save As dialog box

Your folder will differ

Current filename

Files in current folder

Click to save file

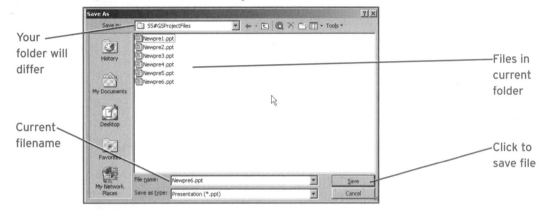

Figure GS-17: New from Existing Presentation dialog box

Your folder will differ

Type new filename here

Files you just created

Click to create a new file from an existing presentation

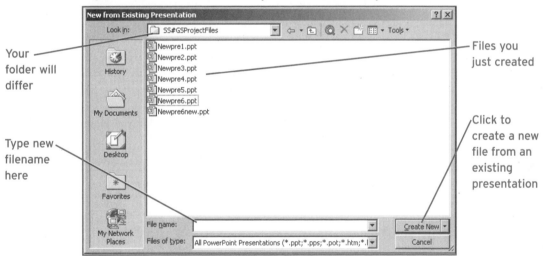

Skill Set

Getting Started with PowerPoint 2002

Target Your Skills

1 Review Figure GS-18 to identify the 12 elements on the PowerPoint screen. Use a sheet of paper to name each element and write a short statement about the function of each.

Figure GS-18

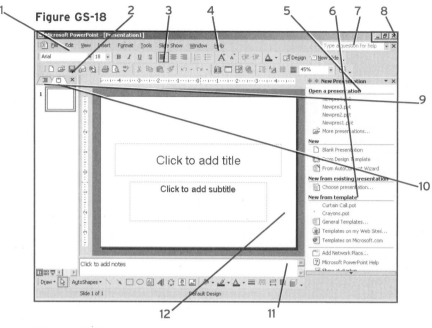

2 Figure GS-19 shows a Help screen that discusses the document recovery feature in PowerPoint. Use the Ask a question box to find this page about document recovery, and then read this screen. Then use the Answer wizard to find out about the new features in PowerPoint 2002. (*Hint*: Search on the keyword "new features".)

Figure GS-19

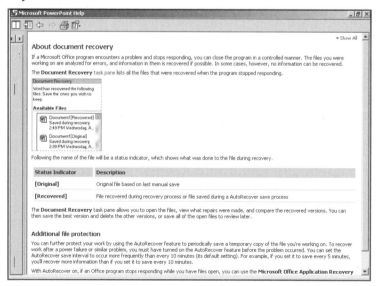

Skill List

1. Create presentations manually and using automated tools
2. Add slides to and delete slides from presentations
3. Modify headers and footers in the Slide Master

When you create a presentation in PowerPoint, you can start "from scratch" by opening a blank presentation, then enter content and create your own design. You can also choose to use the automated tools that come with PowerPoint to create presentations. These automated tools ask you a series of questions about the type of presentation you want to create, such as a marketing plan. Based on your answers, PowerPoint creates a designed presentation containing sample text that you can adapt to suit your needs.

If you're not the artistic type and wonder how you can make your presentations look professional, you can begin by having PowerPoint design the slides for you. PowerPoint can set up the background graphics, colors, and text styles for the presentation, and then you can add your own text. But you don't always need to start a new presentation; PowerPoint makes it easy to adapt existing presentations by deleting slides, creating new ones, or importing slides from other presentations.

When you create presentations, you might want the same text or graphic to appear on every slide. In PowerPoint, you only need to add this information once and indicate which slides you want it applied to.

Skill Set 1
Creating Presentations

Create Presentations Manually and Using Automated Tools
Create Presentations from a Blank Presentation

You can create a PowerPoint presentation by starting from a blank presentation. When you start PowerPoint, a new blank presentation opens. If PowerPoint is already running, you can use the Blank Presentation command in the New Presentation task pane to create a new presentation with one title slide. You can change the slide layout, add new slides, enhance slides with text and graphics, select a design template, animation schemes, or color scheme, then save the presentation.

Step 1
If a new blank presentation is not open, click the New button on the toolbar to open a new blank presentation.

Activity Steps

1. Start PowerPoint (if PowerPoint is already running, click **File** on the menu bar, click **New** to open the task pane, then click **Blank Presentation** on the New Presentation task pane)
   See Figure 1-1.

2. Click **Click to add title**, then type **Broadway Lights Theater**

3. Click **Click to add subtitle**, then type **Staging Broadway on Main Street**

4. Click the **New Slide button** on the toolbar

5. Click **Click to add title**, type **Broadway Lights Theater**, press **[Enter]**, type **Summer of Musicals**, then click **Click to add text**

6. Type **Pippin**, press **[Enter]**, type **A Chorus Line**, press **[Enter]**, type **Hello Dolly**, press **[Enter]**, type **Peter Pan**, press **[Enter]**, then type **Evita**
   See Figure 1-2.

   file close file

Figure 1-1: A new blank presentation

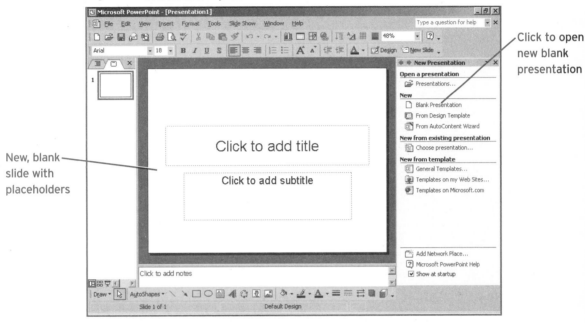

New, blank slide with placeholders

Click to open new blank presentation

Figure 1-2: Presentation with two slides

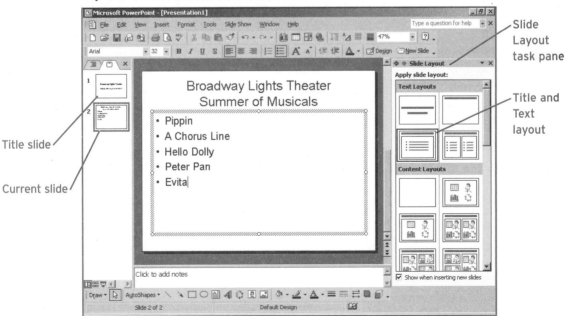

Title slide

Current slide

Slide Layout task pane

Title and Text layout

Skill Set 1

Create Presentations Manually and Using Automated Tools

Create Presentations using the AutoContent Wizard

If you are unsure how to begin creating your presentation, or if you are pressed to meet a deadline, PowerPoint comes with an automated tool that can help you get started. The **AutoContent Wizard** is a series of dialog boxes that asks you to choose your presentation purpose, such as selling a product or recommending a strategy, and how you plan to present it, such as on-screen or over the Web. Based on your answers, the Wizard creates a presentation with sample content and a professional-looking design. You can then adapt the sample text and design to meet your specific needs. While the AutoContent Wizard can save you time and help you create high-quality presentations, you have complete control over the final look and content.

The AutoContent Wizard has five categories of presentations: General, Corporate, Projects, Sales/Marketing, and Carnegie Coach. Click All to see all the presentations for all categories.

Activity Steps

1. Click **File** on the menu bar, then click **New**

2. Click **From AutoContent Wizard** in the New Presentation task pane
   The AutoContent Wizard opens, and the Office Assistant appears.

3. Click **No** on the Office Assistant, then click **Next**
   See Figure 1-3.

4. Click **Carnegie Coach**, click **Motivating A Team**, then click **Next**

5. Click the **On-screen presentation option button** (if not already selected), then click **Next**

6. Click the **Presentation title box**, then type **Teambuilding at Broadway Lights Theater**

7. Press **[Tab]**, type **Confidential** in the Footer box, click the **Slide number check box** to deselect it, then click **Next**

8. Click **Finish**
   The presentation contains 10 predesigned slides with content generated by PowerPoint. *See Figure 1-4.*

 close file

Figure 1-3: AutoContent Wizard Presentation Type dialog box

General presentations are displayed

Click to select from Carnegie Coach presentations

Figure 1-4: Presentation created by AutoContent Wizard

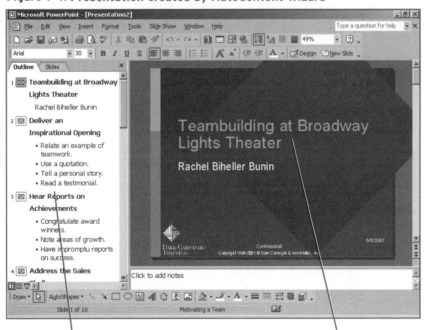

Content supplied by the AutoContent Wizard

Content you supplied through the AutoContent Wizard

Skill Set 1

Creating presentations

Create Presentations Manually and Using Automated Tools

Create Presentations Using Design Templates

A **design template** is a file that offers no suggested text, but does contain all the specifications for how a presentation looks, including background designs, color schemes, fonts, and layout. **Layout** is the organization of text and graphics on a slide. Though PowerPoint comes with more than 30 design templates that you can apply to some or all slides in your presentation, you can also create your own. For example, you could create a custom design template containing your company logo and company colors to be applied to every slide. You could then base future presentations on your customized design template. You can preview and select design templates in the Slide Design task pane.

For your convenience, the Slide Design task pane organizes templates into areas called Recently Used and Used in This Presentation.

Activity Steps

1. Click **File** on the menu bar, click **New**, then click **From Design Template** in the New Presentation task pane

2. In the Slide Design task pane, scroll if necessary until you see the Capsules design template in the Apply a design template area
   The name of each design template appears as a ScreenTip when you place the pointer over the thumbnail of each design template.

3. Click the **Capsules design template**
   See Figure 1-5.

4. Click **Click to add title**, type **Teambuilding at Broadway Lights Theater**, click **Click to add subtitle**, type **Staging Broadway on Main Street**, then click outside the text box to deselect it

5. Scroll the design template list, then click the **Kimono design template**
   See Figure 1-6.

 close file

Figure 1-5: Capsules design template

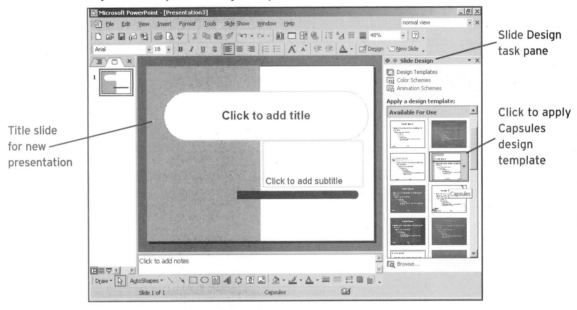

Slide **Design** task **pane**

Title slide for new presentation

Click to **apply** Capsules design template

Figure 1-6: Kimono design template applied

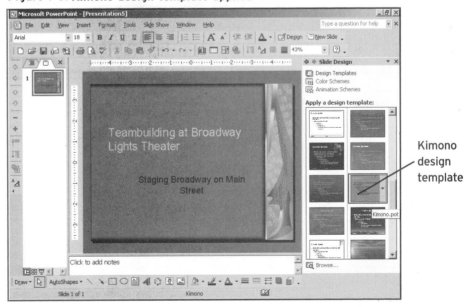

Kimono design template

Skill Set 1

Creating Presentations

Add Slides to and Delete Slides from Presentations

Add Slides to Presentations

As you work on a presentation and add content, you will need to add slides. The New Slide button on the Formatting toolbar adds a new slide after the selected slide. It also displays the Slide Layout task pane, which allows you to choose a layout for the new slide. A layout contains **placeholders**, boxes with dotted or hatchmarked borders, for entering various types of information, such as images, bulleted lists, and charts. Text layouts contain placeholders for titles and bulleted lists. Content layouts contain placeholders for charts, graphics, diagrams, tables, and media clips.

Add a new slide by clicking a slide in the Outline or Slides tab then pressing [Enter]. To add a slide and specify its layout at the same time, click the list arrow next to a slide layout in the Slide Layout task pane, then click Insert New Slide.

Activity Steps

 open Present1.ppt

1. Click Slide 3 on the Slides tab

2. Click the New Slide button on the toolbar
   The new slide (slide 4) is inserted after slide 3, the slide you had selected.

3. Click the Title and 2-Column Text layout in the Slide Layout task pane to apply the layout to the new slide
   See Figure 1-7.

4. Click Click to add title, then type Featured Actors

5. Click Click to add text in the left text box, type Michael Benjamins, press [Enter], type Emily Catalan, press [Enter], type Jennifer Laina, press [Enter], then type David Samuels

6. Click Click to add text in the right text box, type Pippin, press [Enter], type A Chorus Line, press [Enter], type Evita, press [Enter], type Peter Pan, then click the slide to deselect the text box
   See Figure 1-8.

7. Click the Close button on the Slide Layout task pane

close Present1.ppt

extra!

Creating new presentations from existing presentations
You can create a new presentation by using an existing presentation as a base, then adding or modifying slides to adapt the content and design for the new audience. Open the New Presentation task pane, click Choose presentation in the New from existing presentation area of the task pane, open the presentation you want to use, then save it with a new name. You can also use the Save As command on the File menu at any time to save a new version of a presentation with a different name.

Certification Circle

Figure 1-7: Inserting a slide

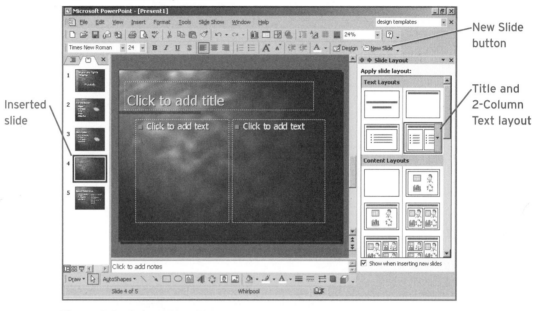

New Slide button

Inserted slide

Title and 2-Column Text layout

Figure 1-8: Completed slide

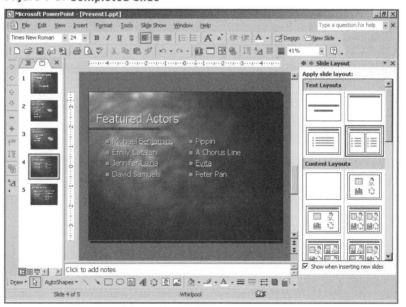

Skill Set 1
Creating Presentations

Add Slides to and Delete Slides from Presentations
Delete Slides from Presentations

There are frequently slides in a presentation that are no longer current, or that you no longer want. You can delete slides easily by selecting them on the Slides or Outline tab, or in Slide Sorter view, then clicking the Delete Slide command on the Edit menu. You can also press [Delete]. To select a group of contiguous slides, click the first slide in the group, press and hold [Shift], then click the last slide in the group. To select non-contiguous slides, press and hold [Ctrl] then click each one.

Often you will want to create a new presentation by deleting slides from an existing presentation. For example, you might have a new project proposal presentation you made for your marketing group that you now want to modify to present to prospective clients. The clients won't need to see the detail slides that an in-house group would need to see.

Step 2
If you delete a slide accidentally, you can retrieve it by immediately clicking the Undo button or pressing [Ctrl] [Z], or by clicking Edit on the menu bar, then clicking Undo Delete Slide.

Activity Steps

 open Present2.ppt

1. Click the **Slide Sorter View button** ⊞, then click **Slide 2** to select the slide you want to delete

2. Press **[Delete]**

3. Click the **Normal View button** ▣

4. Click **Slide 10** on the Slides tab, press and hold **[Ctrl]**, then click **Slide 7** on the Slides tab to select the two slides you want to delete

5. Click **Edit** on the menu bar, then click **Delete Slide** as shown in Figure 1-9

6. Click the **Outline tab**, click **Slide 3** to select the contents of the Mission slide, then press **[Delete]**

 close Present2.ppt

Figure 1-9: Deleting two non-contiguous slides

Delete Slide command

Selected slides to be deleted

Slide Sorter View button

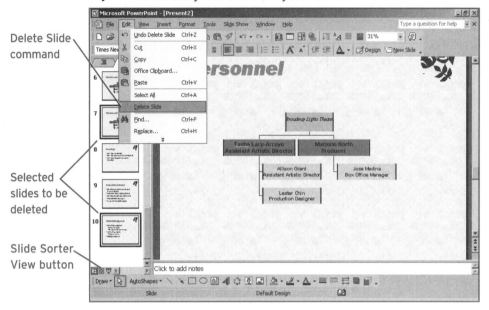

extra!

Copying slides from other presentations

The Slide Finder dialog box makes it possible to copy slides from one presentation to another without having to open the presentation from which you want to copy slides. Click Insert on the menu bar, then click Slides from Files to open the Slide Finder dialog box. Browse to locate the file you want to get the slides from, select the slides you want to copy by clicking the thumbnails in the Select slides area, then click Insert. Click Insert All to copy all the slides from a presentation. Click the Keep source formatting check box to retain the formatting of the source presentation; otherwise the template of the destination file will be applied to the slides. You can even add presentations to the List of Favorites tab if you select slides from a specific presentation often.

Skill Set 1
Creating Presentations

Modify Headers and Footers in the Slide Master
Add Information to the Slide Master

The **slide master** is the part of the presentation that specifies how text and graphics appear on each slide. You can use the slide master to make a global change to your presentation, such as changing the font or bullet style. The slide master stores information about the design template, including placeholder sizes, position, background design, and color schemes. The slide master can store text or graphics that you want to appear in the same place on each slide. To omit the graphics from the slide master from a particular slide, select the slide on the Slides tab, click Format on the menu bar, click Background, then click the Omit background graphics from master check box. There are also masters for the notes and handouts pages that work in the same way as the slide master. Your presentation can have more than one slide master. To insert a new slide master, view the slide master, then click Insert New Slide Master on the toolbar.

Activity Steps

 open Present3.ppt

1. Click **View** on the menu bar, point to **Master**, then click **Slide Master** to view the Slide Master
2. Click **Click to edit Master title style**, click the **Font Color list arrow** , click the middle **Custom Color Blue box** in the second row, click the **Font list arrow** , type **BR** to display fonts beginning with Br, click **Broadway**, then click outside the selection
3. Click the **drama masks clip art**, press and hold [Ctrl], then drag the copy of the clip art to the lower left corner of the Object Area for AutoLayouts placeholder
4. Click the **Format Picture button** on the Picture toolbar (or double-click the image if the Picture toolbar is not open), click the **Size tab** on the Format Picture dialog box, select the number in the Scale Height box, type **20**, then click **OK**
   See Figure 1-10.
5. Click the **Normal View button** , click **Slide 5** on the Slides tab, click **Format** on the menu bar, click **Background**, click the **Omit background graphics from master check box**, then click **Apply**
6. Click the **Slide Sorter View button**
   See Figure 1-11.

 close Present3.ppt

step 2
If the Broadway font is not available to you, click any other font.

Figure 1-10: Changing slide master title, font, style, and type

Slide Master

Slide **Master** toolbar

Format Picture button on the Picture toolbar

Font **style** and color changed

Copied and resized image

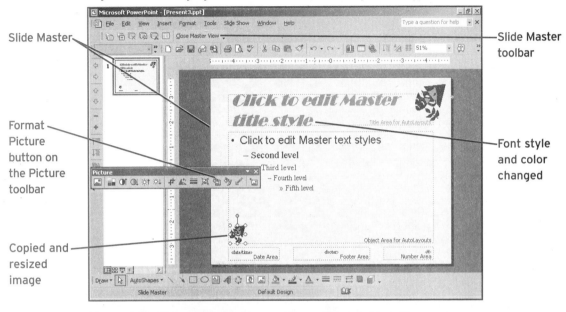

Figure 1-11: Slide showing changes from slide master edits

Graphics from the slide master

Background graphics from slide master not on Slide 5

Font style and color for title changed for all slides

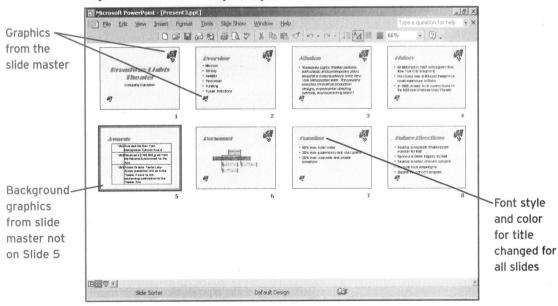

Skill Set 1

Creating Presentations

Modify Headers and Footers in the Slide Master
Add Information to the Footer area of the Slide Master

A **footer** is text information, such as the date, the presentation name, your company name, or the slide number, that appears at the bottom of every slide. You can display a footer on a single slide or on all slides in the presentation. If you display a footer on all slides, you can still exclude it from the title slide. You can add or delete a footer in the Header and Footer dialog box, which you can open from the View menu or from the Options menu in the Print Preview window. A footer automatically becomes part of the slide master.

Activity Steps

 open Present4.ppt

1. Click **View** on the menu bar, click **Header and Footer**, then click the **Slide tab** in the Header and Footer dialog box if it is not already selected

2. Verify that the **Date and time check box** has a check mark in it, then click the **Update automatically option button**

3. Click the **Update Automatically list arrow**, then select the date format **August 20, 2003** (today's date will appear in the list)

4. Make sure the **Slide number check box** is not selected, verify that the **Footer check box** has a check mark in it, then type **Broadway Lights Theater** in the footer box

5. Click the **Don't show on title slide check box** to select it
   See Figure 1-12.

6. Click **Apply to All**, then click **Slide 1** on the Slides tab if it is not already selected

7. Click the **Slide Show (from current slide) button** 🖳, then press **[Spacebar]** to display Slide 2
   See Figure 1-13.

8. Press **[Spacebar]** as many times as necessary to display the rest of the slides in the presentation, then click anywhere to exit the slide show

 close Present4.ppt

If you are using more than one slide master in your presentation, clicking Apply to All applies the footer to all the slide masters in your presentation.

Figure 1-12: Header and Footer dialog box

Current date will display as this date format

Click to apply footer to all slides

Footer will not appear on title slide

Click to apply footer to current slide only

Information will appear in boxes as shown

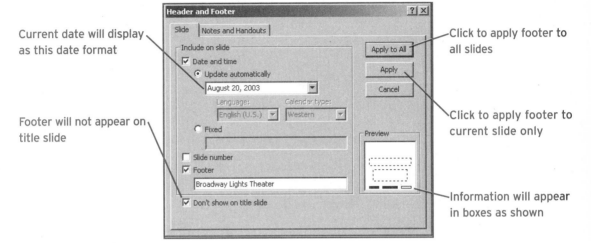

Figure 1-13: Footer on slide

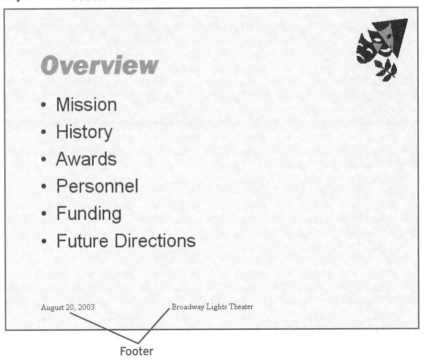

Footer

Skill Set 1

Creating Presentations

Modify Headers and Footers in the Slide Master
Modify Headers and Footers in Handouts and Notes Pages

While you can add only footers to slides, you can add either headers or footers to handouts and notes pages. **Handouts** are copies of your slides that you can provide your audience to help them follow the presentation. **Notes pages** contain a copy of the slides along with notes on what to say about each slide.

Slide numbers on printed notes pages and handouts are called **page numbers** and are contained in the header or footer. You can modify the headers and footers on handouts and notes pages using either Handout Master View or the Notes and Handouts tab in the Header and Footer dialog box. To open Handout Master View, click View on the menu bar, click Master, then click Handout Master. You must show the header or footer on all notes pages or handouts.

If you want to restore the default placeholders to the handout master, open the handout master, delete the placeholder if it has been removed or resized, click Format on the menu bar, click Handout Master Layout, then click the Placeholder check box to restore.

Activity Steps

 open Present5.ppt

1. Click **View** on the menu bar, click **Header and Footer**, then click the **Notes and Handouts tab**

2. Verify that the **Date and time check box** is selected, then click the **Update automatically option button**

3. Verify that the **Header check box** is selected, then type **Broadway Lights Theater Patrons' Dinner** in the Header box

4. Verify that the **Page number check box** is selected, verify that the **Footer check box** is selected, click the **Footer box**, then type **Thank you for your continued support!**
   See Figure 1-14.

5. Click **Apply to All**

6. Click **View** on the menu bar, click **Notes Page**, click the **Zoom list arrow**, then click **Fit** to view the header and footer
   See Figure 1-15.

 close Present5.ppt

Figure 1-14: Notes and Handouts tab of Header and Footer dialog box

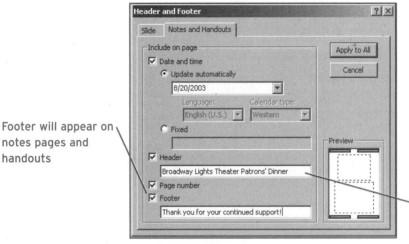

Footer will appear on notes pages and handouts

Header will appear on notes pages and handouts

Figure 1-15: Notes page with header and footer

Header

Date

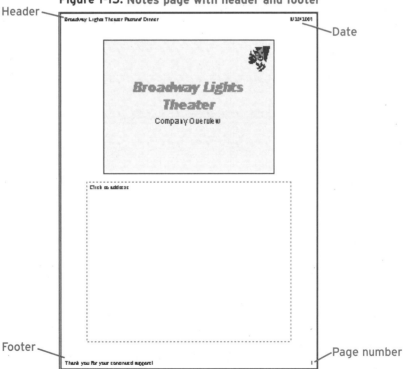

Footer

Page number

Skill Set 1

Inserting and Modifying Text

Target Your Skills

1 Use Figure 1-16 as a guide. Use the AutoContent Wizard to create a Brainstorming session on-screen presentation. Title it **Fundraising Event for Dumont District Band**, add a footer that contains your name, the slide number, and no date. Add your name to the footer in the handout master.

Figure 1-16

Mountain top design template

📁 **Present7.ppt**

2 Use Figure 1-17 as a guide to create a presentation. Add a footer to all the slides containing the text **Broadway Lights Theater** and today's date, updated automatically. Add the text **Staging Broadway on Main Street** as a Header and your name as the Footer to the Notes and Handouts Master.

Figure 1-17

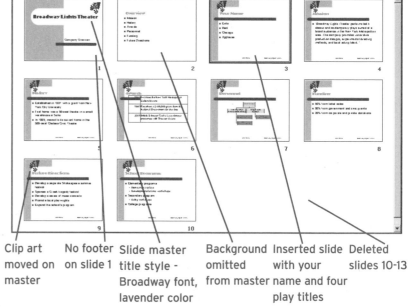

Clip art moved on master

No footer on slide 1

Slide master title style - Broadway font, lavender color

Background omitted from master

Inserted slide with your name and four play titles

Deleted slides 10-13

Skill List

1. Import text from Word
2. Insert, format, and modify text

In PowerPoint, there are many ways to add text and change the way it looks on a slide. You can manually enter text in placeholders, text boxes, as WordArt, or in AutoShapes on individual slides. If you want the same text to appear on every slide of your presentation, you can enter it on the slide master. You can type text directly in PowerPoint or import it from another program such as Word. If you are planning to create a presentation that includes a lot of text, you might want to use **Microsoft Word** or a text editor to write the text. PowerPoint makes it easy to insert Word documents (.doc files), files saved as Rich Text Format (.rtf files), and plain text files (.txt files) into your presentations. When you insert a Word or .rtf file, PowerPoint creates slides with titles and bulleted lists in text boxes based on the heading styles in the document.

Once you insert text in a presentation, you can modify it in several ways. You can edit it to make your message clearer and to correct grammatical or spelling errors. Formatting text helps you emphasize or deemphasize specific words or phrases as well as enhance the appearance of your slides.

Skill Set 2

Inserting and Modifying Text

Import Text from Word
Open a Word Outline as a Presentation

If you created a Word document using Outline formatting, it is very easy to create slides from it using the Insert Slides from Outline Command. When you insert a text file, Tab codes and heading styles define how the text appears on a slide. Text preceded by one tab appears as a slide title; text preceded by two tabs appears as a second level of text, and so on. Text with the Heading 1 style will appear as a title on a slide, text with the Heading 2 style will be the first level of text in a bulleted list, and so on. If the source document contains no styles, PowerPoint creates the outline based on paragraphs and gives each paragraph its own slide.

Activity Steps

1. Start PowerPoint with a blank new presentation on the screen

2. Click **Insert** on the menu bar, then click **Slides from Outline**

3. Click the **Look in list arrow**, navigate to the drive and folder where your Project Files are stored, click **Outline1.doc**, then click **Insert**
   The document file had two heading 1 text entries, each with four heading 2 lines of text. When brought into PowerPoint, two slides were created, as shown in Figure 2-1, one for each heading 1.

4. Close the task pane, click the **Outline tab**, click **View** on the menu bar, point to **Toolbars**, then click **Outlining** (if it's not already selected) to open the Outlining toolbar

5. Click the **Collapse button** ▭ on the Outlining toolbar to collapse the bullets beneath the November recipes head, then click the **Expand button** ✚ to display the bullets again

6. Click the **Collapse All button** ▤ on the Outlining toolbar
   The outlines collapse and you see only the heading 1 text for both slides. *See Figure 2-2.*

    close the open presentation

Step 3
If you get a message telling you that PowerPoint needs a converter to display this file correctly, click Yes to install it.

Figure 2-1: Importing a Word outline

Title slide is blank

Two new slides

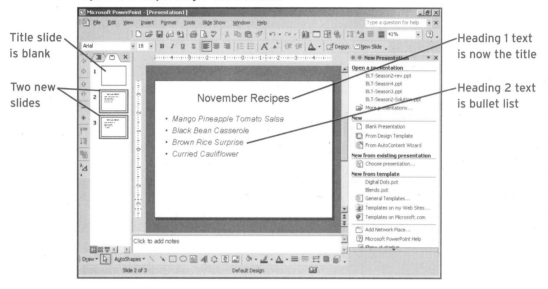

Heading 1 text is now the title

Heading 2 text is bullet list

Figure 2-2: Using the Outline tab

Outline tab

Slide icon

Collapse button

Expand button

Collapse All button

Expand All button

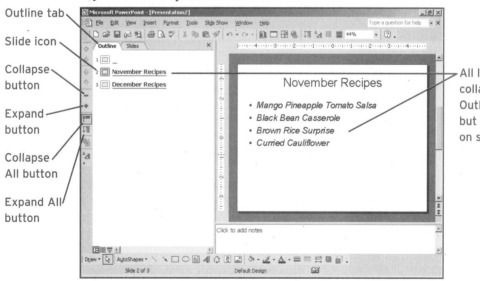

All levels are collapsed on Outline tab but visible on slide

Skill Set 2
Inserting and Modifying Text

Insert, Format, and Modify Text
Add Body or Title Text to Slides

Inserting text onto slides is a critical part of creating a presentation. There are many ways to insert text onto a slide, one of which is through slide layouts. PowerPoint provides four different slide layouts appropriate for text. To insert text, click the placeholder, then start typing. If your text won't fit into the current layout, you can choose a different layout that has additional text placeholders. When you change the slide layout to add a text placeholder, the text will have the formatting specified by the default placeholders.

Activity Steps

 open Recipes1.ppt

1. Click **Slide 2**, click **View** on the menu bar, click **Task Pane**, click the **Other Task Panes list arrow** on the task pane, click **Slide Layout** (if it is not already selected), then click the **Title and 2-Column Text** icon in the Text Layouts area of the task pane
   The existing text is now formatted in the left text placeholder, and a new placeholder with a bullet list appears on the right, ready for you to enter text.

2. Click **Click to add text**, type **Cherry compote**, press **[Enter]**, type **Apple crumble**, press **[Enter]**, type **Apple cobbler**, press **[Enter]**, type **Cucumber salad**, then click anywhere on the slide
   See Figure 2-3.

3. Click **Slide 3** on the Outline tab, click the **New Slide button** on the toolbar, click **Click to add title**, type **January Recipes**, click **Click to add text**, type **Baked Alaska**, press **[Enter]**, type **Black Bean Soup**, press **[Enter]**, then type **Manicotti**
   All text entered in placeholders appears on the Outline tab.

4. Click **Slide 1** on the Outline tab, click the **New Slide button** on the toolbar, click the **Title Slide layout** in the Text Layouts task pane, click **Click to add title**, type **Steven's favorite dishes**, click **Click to add subtitle**, then type **CJ says, "It's the best!"**

5. Collapse the outline for the November and December Recipes slides, then click **Slide 5**
   See Figure 2-4.

 close Recipes1.ppt

> **tip**
>
> You can delete, insert, cut, copy, and paste slides directly from the Outline tab; right-click any slide for a complete list of options.

Figure 2-3: Adding text by changing the slide layout

Second text box identified in Outline view

Other Task Panes list arrow

Title and 2-Column Text layout

Text added to second column

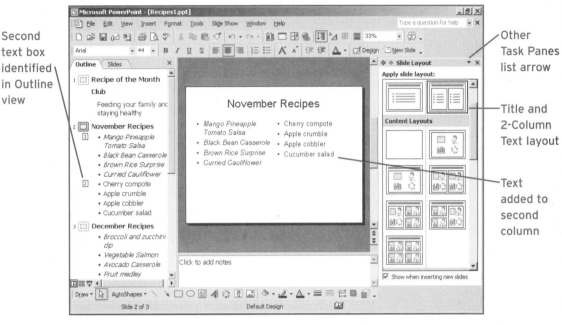

Figure 2-4: Adding two new slides with text layouts

New slides

Title Slide layout

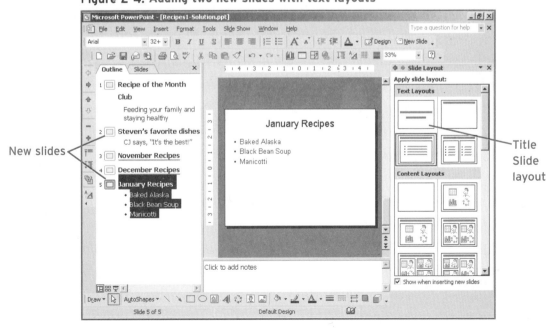

Microsoft PowerPoint 2002 **43**

Skill Set 2

Inserting and Modifying Text

Insert, Format, and Modify Text
Add Text boxes to Slides

You can add text anywhere on a slide by using the Text Box button. However, keep in mind that text added with the Text Box button does not appear in the Outline tab, although you can see it on the Slide tab. If you want the text inside a text box to stay on one line, click the Text Box button, click where you want to place the text, then start typing. The text box will expand to fit the text until you press [Enter] or stop typing. If you want the text box to be a specific size, click the Text Box button, drag to create a text box to the size you want, then start typing. When the text reaches the end of a line, it will wrap to the next line.

Activity Steps

 open DecJan1.ppt

1. Click **December Recipes** in the Outline tab, then close the task pane if it is open

2. Click the **Text Box button** on the Drawing toolbar, click near the lower-right corner of the December Recipes slide, then type **Happy Holidays!**
See Figure 2-5.

Step 3
To open the Ruler, click View on the menu bar, then click Ruler.

3. Click the **January Recipes slide**, click the **Text Box button** on the Drawing toolbar, then drag a text box under the M in Manicotti that is 4" wide using the horizontal ruler as a guide

4. Type **Happy New Year to all our gourmet friends. We will not be meeting in February but will meet again in March with more delicious recipes for you to learn how to cook!**
See Figure 2-6.

 close DecJan1.ppt

Figure 2-5: Adding a text box

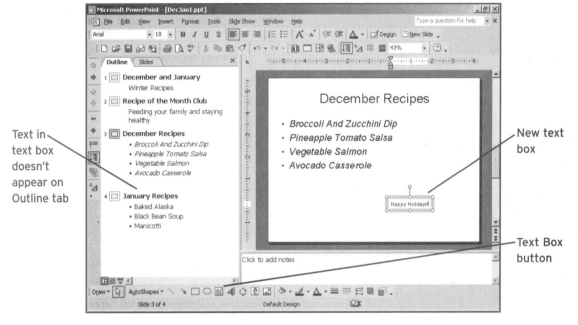

Text in text box doesn't appear on Outline tab

New text box

Text Box button

Figure 2-6: Text box with wrapped text

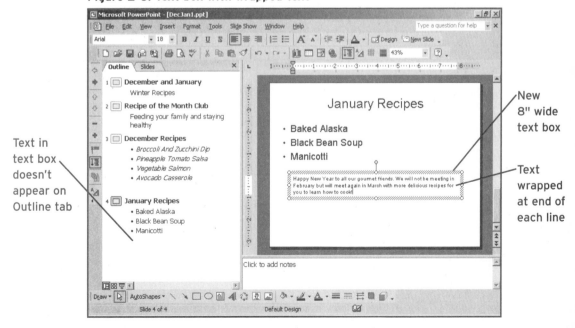

Text in text box doesn't appear on Outline tab

New 8" wide text box

Text wrapped at end of each line

Skill Set 2

Inserting and Modifying Text

Insert, Format, and Modify Text
Add Text to an AutoShape

If you want your words to have more visual impact, you can place them inside a graphic. **AutoShapes** are a group of ready-made graphics that come with PowerPoint, and include basic shapes such as squares and circles as well as elaborate shapes such as banners, stars, symbols, and connectors. To add text to a new AutoShape, begin typing as soon as you draw the shape. To add text to an existing AutoShape, click to select the AutoShape then type the text. Any text you add to an AutoShape automatically becomes part of the AutoShape. The image combined with the text helps emphasize your message.

Activity Steps

 open DecJan2.ppt

Double-click the AutoShape to open the Format AutoShape dialog box to change its colors and lines, size, position, and text box specifications. If this slide is part of a Web page, you can also specify alternative text to display as the graphic is loading.

1. Click **December Recipes** in the Outline tab, click **AutoShapes** on the Drawing toolbar, point to **Stars and Banners**, then click **Explosion2** (the second icon)

2. Click slightly below and to the right of Casserole on the December Recipes slide, type **Happy Holidays!**, drag the corner handles of the AutoShape so the whole text is visible inside the shape, then click the slide to deselect the AutoShape
See Figure 2-7.

3. Click **January Recipes** in the Outline tab, click **AutoShapes** on the Drawing toolbar, point to **Callouts**, then click **Rectangular Callout** (the first icon)
Callouts have an additional yellow sizing handle that resizes the arrow part of the AutoShape.

4. Click to the right of Black Bean Soup, drag the shape up and to the right, stopping just under the word Recipes, type **Steven says, "Black Bean Soup is delicious!"**, then click outside the AutoShape to deselect the AutoShape callout
Your screen should look like Figure 2-8.

 close DecJan2.ppt

Figure 2-7: Adding text with an AutoShape

AutoShape text is not on Outline tab

AutoShapes button

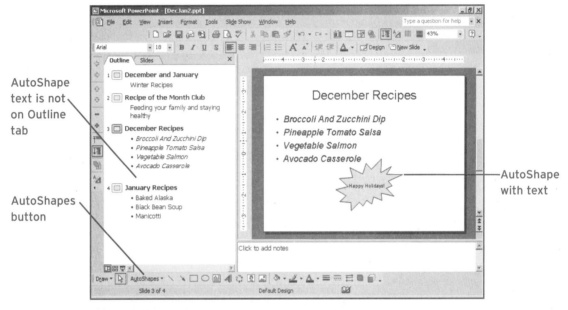

AutoShape with text

Figure 2-8: Adding a callout

AutoShape text is not on Outline tab

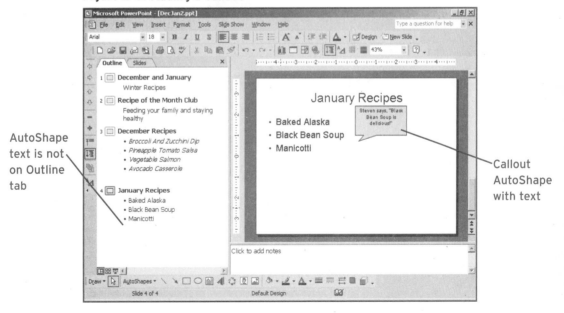

Callout AutoShape with text

Skill Set 2

Inserting and Modifying Text

Insert, Format, and Modify Text
Add WordArt

Another way to give your words more visual impact is to transform them into **WordArt**. WordArt is a text object that has highly stylized effects, including color, outline, shape, shading, font, sizes, and fill. WordArt is best used for single words or short phrases on a slide. Text added as WordArt does not appear on the Outline tab. You insert WordArt using the WordArt button on the Drawing toolbar.

Selected WordArt has sizing handles as well as a green rotation handle at the top that you can drag to rotate the WordArt to any angle.

Activity Steps

 open DecJan3.ppt

1. Click **Slide 4**, then click the **Insert WordArt button** 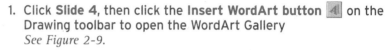 on the Drawing toolbar to open the WordArt Gallery
   See Figure 2-9.

2. Click **Rainbow WordArt style** in the third row in the fourth column, then click **OK**

3. Type **Happy New Year**, click the **Font list arrow**, click **Comic Sans MS**, click the **Bold button** , then click **OK**

4. Use the pointer to drag the **WordArt object** to below the text in the center of the slide
   See Figure 2-10.

 close DecJan3.ppt

Figure 2-9: WordArt Gallery dialog box

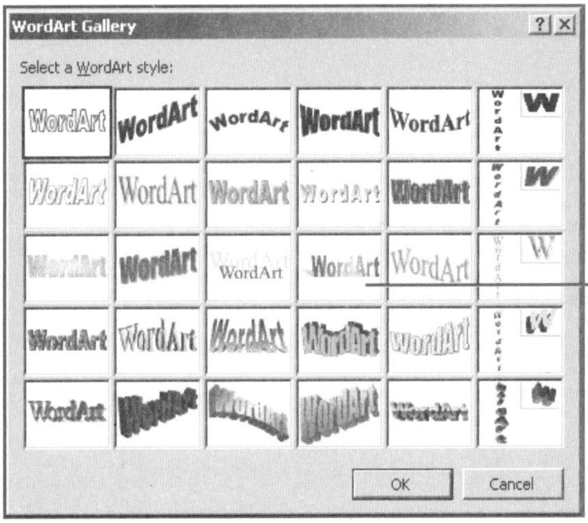

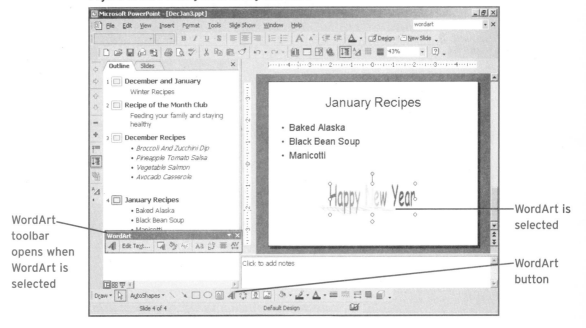

Click this style

Figure 2-10: Adding text using WordArt

WordArt toolbar opens when WordArt is selected

WordArt is selected

WordArt button

Skill Set 2

Inserting and Modifying Text

Insert, Format, and Modify text
Edit Text on Slides

Whether you insert a document file into PowerPoint to create slides or begin typing text directly in PowerPoint, you will probably want to make changes to the text to fix errors or make your message stronger. In Normal view you can edit directly on the slides or on the Outline tab.

You can add and delete words in bulleted lists, add new bullets, or move and rearrange the order of bulleted lists. You can change words or correct spelling errors. Using the copy and paste commands, you can copy words or phrases from one place to another on the same slide or to other slides.

Activity Steps

 open Recipes2.ppt

1. Click the **November Recipes slide** on the Outline tab
2. Click to the right of the **c** in **compote** in the Outline tab, press **[Backspace]**, type **C**, click to the right of the **c** in **crumble** in the Outline tab, press **[Backspace]**, then type **C**
   You can also edit text directly on a slide.
3. Double-click **cobbler** on the slide, type **Pie**, click to the right of the **s** in **salad** on the slide, press **[Backspace]**, then type **S**
   The slide for November should look similar to Figure 2-11.
4. Place the pointer to the left of **Fruit medley** on slide 3 in the Outline tab so that the pointer changes to ⊕, click to select **Fruit medley**, then press **[Del]**
5. Place the pointer to the left of **Mango Pineapple** on slide 2 on the Outline tab, click to select the whole line, click the **Copy button** on the toolbar, click below **Avocado** on slide 3 on the Outline tab, then click the **Paste button** on the toolbar
   The line is copied from one slide to another.
6. Double-click **Mango** on slide 3 in the Outline tab, press **[Del]**, place the pointer to the left of **Pineapple** on slide 3 so that the pointer changes to ⊕, press and hold the left mouse button, then drag **Pineapple Tomato Salsa** up so that it is below **Broccoli**, as shown in Figure 2-12

tip

Avoid putting too much text on a slide. Try to limit each slide to six bulleted items and a maximum of six words per bulleted item.

extra!

Using Find and Replace

If there is a word that you want to change globally, click Edit on the menu bar, then click Replace to open the Replace dialog box. Type the word you want to find in the Find what box, then type the word you want to replace it with in the Replace with box. You can specify whether to search for whole words only or match the case for the text you want to find. Click Find Next to begin the operation. Click Replace if you want to confirm each replacement one by one. Click Replace All to replace all occurrences throughout the presentation.

Figure 2-11: Editing text on a slide

Edited text

Edited text

Figure 2-12: Moving text

Bullet item being moved

New bullet item

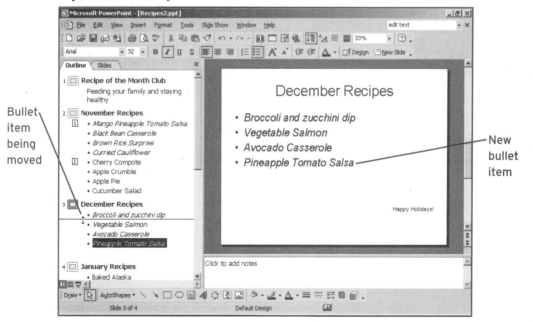

Skill Set 2

Inserting and Modifying Text

Insert, Format, and Modify Text
Format Text on Slides

You can take advantage of PowerPoint's many formatting features to enhance the appearance of text and help convey your message clearly. You can use bold formatting to emphasize certain words, bright colors to communicate a cheerful mood, or somber colors to convey a serious message.

You should use formatting wisely and with consideration for your audience. You can apply a design template to your presentation and then modify the formatting to meet your needs. Even though you have many choices, you should limit your use of font styles and formatting to avoid creating a presentation that is in poor taste or so busy that your message gets lost in the clutter. If possible, limit number of fonts to two and vary size, weight, and other attributes for subtle emphasis. PowerPoint provides design templates that offer preset fonts, color schemes, and layouts to ensure a unified look throughout your presentation.

Activity Steps

 open Recipes3.ppt

1. Click **View** on the menu bar, click **Task Pane**, click the **Other Task Panes list arrow**, click **Slide Design - Design Templates**, then click the **Capsules design template**
2. Close the **Slide Design** task pane, drag the pointer to select **Recipe of the Month Club** on slide 1, click the **Font list arrow** on the Formatting toolbar, click **Broadway**, click the **Font Size list arrow**, then click **40** (If Broadway is not available, choose another font)
3. Select **Feeding your family and staying healthy**, click the **Italic button** , click the **Font Color list arrow**, click the **lavender square** (the right-most square in the row), then click outside the selection
   See Figure 2-13.
4. Click **Slide 3** on the Slides tab, click the **Happy Holidays text box** to select it, then click the **text box border** with the Move pointer so that the text box has a dotted border
5. Click the **Increase Font Size button** three times so that the font size is **28**, drag the text box to the left so it is positioned on the slide, click the **Shadow button**, then click the **Font Color button** to change the color to lavender
6. Click the **Slide Sorter View button**, click the **Zoom list arrow** on the Slide Sorter toolbar, then click **100%**
   Your slides should look similar to Figure 2-14.

 close Recipes3.ppt

Step 1
You can also click the Slide Design button to open the Slide Design task pane.

Figure 2-13: Applying formatting, font styles, and font colors

Font Color list arrow

Increase Font Size button

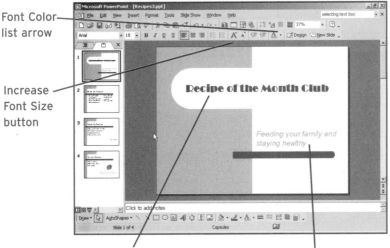

Text formatted with
Broadway font, 40-point

Text formatted with
italic and lavender color

Figure 2-14: Finished presentation

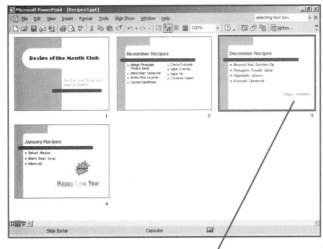

Reformatted text

Replacing fonts throughout a presentation

If you want to replace all text that is in one font with another font throughout a presentation, click Format on the menu bar, click Replace Fonts, click the Replace drop down list arrow, select the font to replace, click the With drop down list arrow to select the font you want to replace it with, then click Replace. You can select the text that is in the font you want to replace before clicking Format on the menu bar to have that font appear in the Replace text box automatically. All occurrences of the font throughout the presentation will be replaced. To change the case of selected text to Sentence, Lower, Upper, Title, or Toggle case, click Format on the menu bar, click Change Case, click the Case option button, then click OK.

Skill Set 2

Inserting and Modifying Text

Target Your Skills

1 Use Figure 2-15 as a guide to create a presentation. Start with a new blank presentation, then insert slides from the Outline file Outline2.doc. Save the presentation as Outline2.ppt. Apply the Blends design template to all the slides. **open**

open Aviva1.ppt

2 Use Figure 2-16 as a guide to create a final presentation. Format the placeholder text as shown.

Figure 2-15   Blends design template

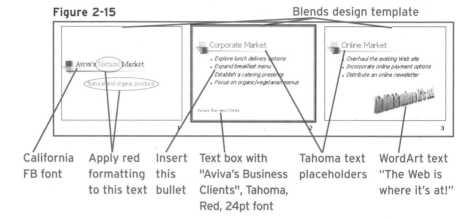

California FB font | Apply red formatting to this text | Insert this bullet | Text box with "Aviva's Business Clients", Tahoma, Red, 24pt font | Tahoma text placeholders | WordArt text "The Web is where it's at!"

Figure 2-16

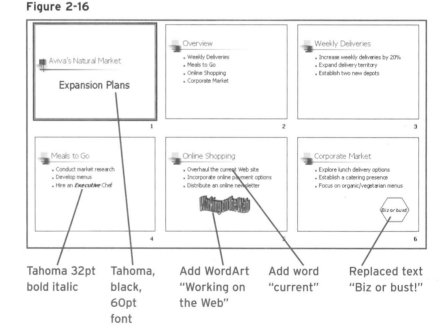

Tahoma 32pt bold italic | Tahoma, black, 60pt font | Add WordArt "Working on the Web" | Add word "current" | Replaced text "Biz or bust!"

Skill Set 3

Skill List

1. Add tables, charts, clip art, and bitmap images to slides
2. Customize slide backgrounds
3. Add OfficeArt elements to slides
4. Apply custom formats to tables

Most people absorb information and concepts better from a presentation when images are used to complement text. In this skill set, you will learn how to add photographs, images, and other graphic objects such as organization charts to slides. You will learn to apply slide backgrounds that contain textures, patterns, and images. You will learn to present numerical data in your presentation as a chart so that your audience can quickly grasp its meaning. PowerPoint uses a program called Microsoft Graph to create charts. A **chart** is a graphic presentation of data, useful for showing trends or comparisons. You will also learn to create **tables**, which are structures that organize data in columns and rows, and then learn how to format tables to make them visually interesting.

Skill Set 3

Inserting and Modifying Visual Elements

Add Tables, Charts, Clip Art, and Bitmap Images to Slides

Create Tables on Slides

Some text or graphic information is best presented as a **table**, which is made up of columns and rows. The basic unit of a table is a **cell**, the intersection of a column and row. In a PowerPoint slide, you can insert a table with any number of columns and rows and then enter text or insert images into the individual cells. Typically you use the first row of a table to identify the content of each column; these are the **column heads**. You can also insert **row labels** into each cell of the first column to identify the content of each row.

The Title and Table layout on the Slide Layout task pane makes it easy to add a table to a slide. You can also insert a table by clicking the Insert Table button on the Standard toolbar, or by clicking Insert on the menu bar, then clicking Table. You specify the number of columns and rows in the Insert Table dialog box.

Activity Steps

 open Bwayshk1.ppt

You can divide an existing column or row by using the Draw Table button on the Tables and Borders toolbar. Click the Draw Table button, then draw a line between any two columns or rows. To create a new row at the bottom of the table, place the insertion point in the cell in the last row and column, then press [Tab].

1. Click **View** on the menu bar, click **Task Pane** to open the task pane, click the **Other Task Panes down arrow**, then click **Slide Layout**
2. Click **Slide 2** to display the slide with the Title and Text layout, then scroll down the Slide Layout task pane until you see the Other Layouts section
3. Click the **Title and Table layout** in the Other Layouts section to change the layout of slide 2
   See Figure 3-1.
4. Double-click **Double click to add table**, type **4** in the Number of columns box, press [Tab], type **3** in the Number of rows box, then click **OK**
   The Tables and Borders toolbar opens.
5. Close the task pane, click **Click to add title**, then type **Ticket Prices**
6. Click the first cell in the upper left corner, press [Tab] to move to row 1 column 2, type **Child**, press [Tab], type **Student**, press [Tab], type **Adult**, then press [Tab] to move to row 2
7. Type **Afternoon**, press [Tab], type **$5**, press [Tab], type **$7**, press [Tab], type **$10**, press [Tab] to move to row 3, type **Evening**, press [Tab], type **$6**, press [Tab], type **$8**, press [Tab], type **$15** then click the slide outside the table
   The Tables and Borders toolbar closes and the table is complete. *See Figure 3-2.*

 close Bwayshk1.ppt

Figure 3-1: Title and Table layout applied

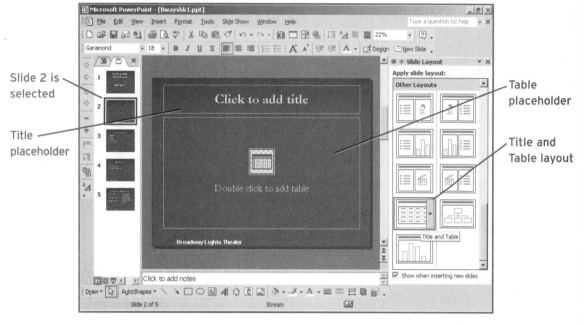

Slide 2 is selected

Title placeholder

Table placeholder

Title and Table layout

Figure 3-2: Table in slide

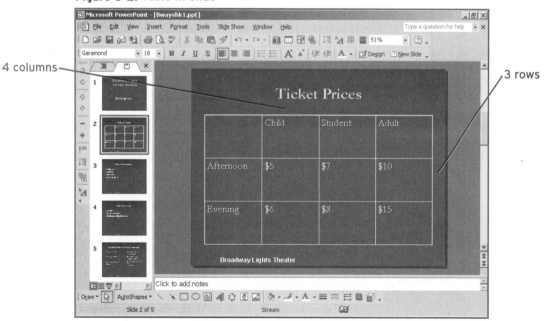

4 columns

3 rows

Skill Set 3
Inserting and Modifying Visual Elements

Add Tables, Charts, Clip Art, and Bitmap Images to Slides
Add Clip Art Images to Slides

A presentation would be pretty dull if it contained only words. Fortunately, Office XP comes with a large library of drawings, images, photographs, sounds, and other media files, all of which are called **clips**. Clips are stored and organized in a repository called the **Clip Organizer**. **Clip art** is a collection of images in the Clip Organizer that you can use to enhance your presentations. You can browse through the clip collections using the search feature in the Insert Clip Art task pane.

You can also use the Insert Clip Art task pane to browse for **AutoShapes**, which are ready-made shapes provided by Office XP that you can insert into your presentations.

When you insert a clip, you see an Automatic Layout SmartTag. If you click the Automatic Layout Options list arrow, you can stop the automatic layout and have the image appear in the middle of the slide, so you can place it wherever you want.

Activity Steps

 open Bwayshk2.ppt

1. Click **Slide 3** on the Slides tab, click **Insert** on the menu bar, point to **Picture**, then click **Clip Art** (if the Add Clips to Organizer dialog box appears, click **Later**)

2. Type **Shakespeare** in the Search text box in the Insert Clip Art task pane, click **Search**, then click the image of **William Shakespeare** that appears in the Search results (if you don't see William Shakespeare, type **Theater** in the Search text box, then click one of the images that appears)
   See Figure 3-3.

3. Click **Slide 4** on the Slides tab, click the **AutoShapes button** on the Drawing toolbar, then click **More AutoShapes**
   The Insert Clip Art task pane changes to display a selection of AutoShapes.

4. Click the **Cloud image**, then drag it to the lower right corner of the slide
   See Figure 3-4.

 close Bwayshk2.ppt

Figure 3-3: Insert Clip Art task pane search results

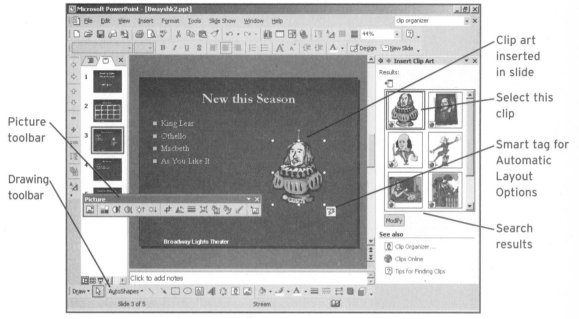

Picture toolbar

Drawing toolbar

Clip art inserted in slide

Select this clip

Smart tag for Automatic Layout Options

Search results

Figure 3-4: AutoShapes in Clip Art task pane

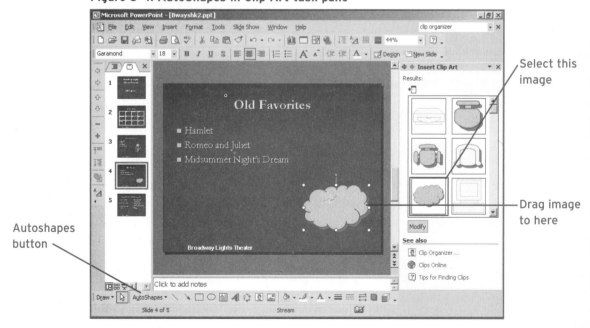

Autoshapes button

Select this image

Drag image to here

Skill Set 3

Inserting and Modifying Visual Elements

Add Tables, Charts, Clip Art, and Bitmap Images to Slides
Add Charts to Slides

You can easily insert a chart into a slide by choosing one of the chart layouts on the Slide Layout task pane. When you insert a chart, Graph opens and displays a chart with a datasheet containing placeholder information. A **datasheet**, which looks like a spreadsheet, is made up of lettered columns and numbered rows, which intersect to form cells. You enter data for the chart by replacing the placeholder text and numbers in the datasheet. You enter the **data series**, or the information that is represented in the chart, in the datasheet rows. Each data series has a unique color. Pie charts have only one data series. The **categories** of data are represented along the horizontal or **X-axis** of the chart; the **values** of data are represented along the vertical or **Y-axis**.

Activity Steps

 open Bwayshk3.ppt

1. Click **Slide 2**, then click the **Insert Chart button** on the content layout placeholder
   See Figure 3-5.

2. Click the **East** cell, type **Classics**, press [Tab], type **125**, press [Tab], type **132**, press [Tab], type **150**, press [Tab], then type **250**

3. Click the **West** cell, type **Musicals**, press [Tab], type **175**, press [Tab], type **250**, press [Tab], type **295**, press [Tab], then type **310**

4. Click the **North** cell, type **Comedies**, press [Tab], type **160**, press [Tab], type **140**, press [Tab], type **210**, press [Tab], then type **285**

5. Close the datasheet, double-click **300** on the Value Axis, click the **Number tab**, click **Currency** in the Category list box, type **0** in the Decimal places list box, then click **OK**

6. Click **Chart** on the menu bar, click **Chart Type**, click **Line** in the Chart type list box, click **OK** to view the data as a line graph, click **Chart** on the menu bar, click **Chart Type**, click **Column**, click the **Stacked Column icon** (first row, second column) in the Chart Sub-type list box, then click **OK**

7. Double-click the **Legend**, click **Fill Effects**, click the **Texture tab**, click the **Paper Bag effect**, click **OK**, then click **OK** again

8. Click **Click to add title**, then type **Ticket Sales in Hundreds of Dollars**
   See Figure 3-6.

 close Bwayshk3.ppt

Step 7
The Chart Objects list box on the Standard toolbar tells you which object in the chart is selected. Click the Chart Objects list arrow to select any object in the chart.

Figure 3-5: Chart with sample data

Datasheet with sample data

Labels identify data series

Y-axis values

X-axis labels

Legend describes each data series

North data series

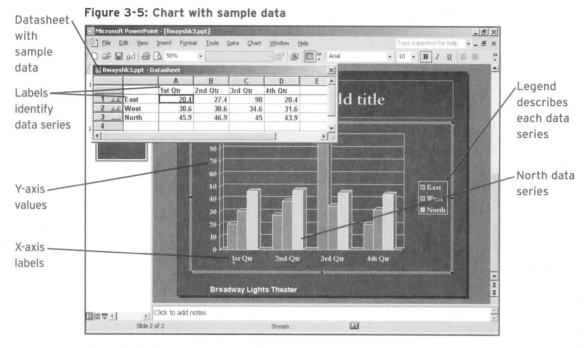

Figure 3-6: Completed chart slide

Value Axis formated in currency with no decimal places

Formatted legend

Stacked column chart

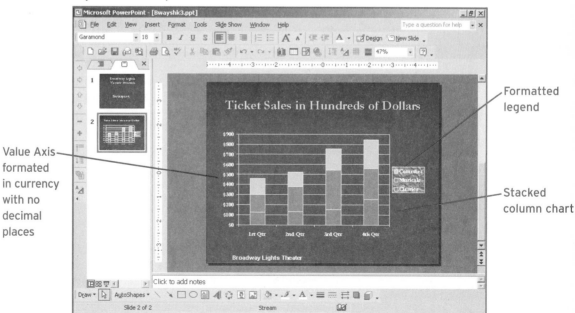

Skill Set 3
Inserting and Modifying Visual Elements

Add Tables, Charts, Clip Art, and Bitmap Images to Slides
Add Bitmap Images to Slides

Although PowerPoint comes loaded with a wide range of clip art images, you will sometimes want to insert other images in your presentation, such as a logo or photograph. A **bitmap image** is an image stored as a series of small dots. The most common bitmap image file format is .bmp, but others are .jpg, .tif, .png, and .gif. You can acquire photographs by taking them using a digital camera, scanning existing pictures using a scanner, or downloading them from a Web site or from a CD of photographs purchased from a commercial retailer. Always keep in mind that most images have some form of copyright protection; take care to honor those rights when you use photos or images in your presentations. To insert a picture that's stored on a disk, you use the Insert Picture command or click the Insert Picture button on the Drawing toolbar. Once you've inserted a picture, you can resize it by using the Format Picture dialog box or by dragging one of the sizing handles. You can move the picture on the slide by dragging it.

Activity Steps

 open Bwayshk4.ppt

1. Click **Slide 2**, click **Insert** on the menu bar, point to **Picture**, then click **From File**

2. Click the **Look in list arrow** to locate your Project Files, click **stars1.jpg**, then click **Insert**

You can double-click a picture to open the Format Picture dialog box.

3. Click **Format** on the menu bar, click **Picture**, click the **Size tab** in the Format Picture dialog box, select the number in the Size and rotate Height box, type **4.0**, verify that the Lock aspect ratio box has a check mark, then press **[Tab]**
   The Width measurement automatically changes in proportion to the height you specified so that the picture keeps the same scale.

4. Click **OK**, click the **Insert Picture button** [icon] on the Drawing toolbar, click **stars2.jpg**, then click **Insert**

5. Position the pointer over the top left sizing handle of stars2.jpg until it changes to a ↖, then drag it up and to the left so that the picture is slightly larger than stars1.jpg

6. Position the pointer over the stars2.jpg image until the pointer changes ⌖, drag the image to the far right of the slide, then drag the stars1.jpg image to the position shown in Figure 3-7 on the slide

 close Bwayshk4.ppt

Figure 3-7: Bitmap images inserted on slide

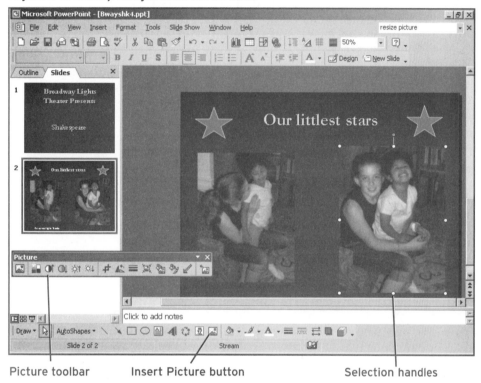

Picture toolbar   Insert Picture button   Selection handles

extra!

Compressing images

Image files are often large; a presentation that includes many images makes for an extremely large PowerPoint file. You can reduce the size of the image files in your PowerPoint presentation by clicking the Compress Pictures button ▣ on the Picture toolbar. The Compress Pictures dialog box lets you specify whether to compress all the pictures in the presentation or just the selected pictures. You can also change the resolution or delete cropped areas. Compression does not reduce the image measurements, only the size of the image file.

Skill Set 3

Inserting and Modifying Visual Elements

Customize Slide Backgrounds
Add Fill Effects to Slide Backgrounds

You can enhance the way a slide looks by applying a **background**, which can apply to all the slides in a presentation or just to selected slides. You can have a solid color background or you can apply one of PowerPoint's special effects, called **fill effects**. You use the Format Background dialog box to apply backgrounds to your slides. You use the Fill Effects dialog box to apply special effects to your backgrounds.

To create customized fill effects on your slide background, click the Gradient tab of the Fill Effects dialog box, choose either one color or two colors in the color area, then select one of the six available shading styles.

Activity Steps

 open Bwayshk5.ppt

1. Click **Format** on the menu bar, click **Background**, click the **Background fill list arrow**, then click **Fill Effects**

2. Click the **Texture tab**, then click **Granite**
   See Figure 3-8.

3. Click **OK**, then click **Apply to all** in the Background dialog box
   See Figure 3-9.

 close Bwayshk5.ppt

extra!

Creating a photo album
If your presentation contains mostly photographs, PowerPoint can automatically create a presentation in the style of a photo album directly from the pictures you select. You can format the album with design templates and select attractive layouts to display your photographs to full advantage. Start a new presentation, click Insert on the menu bar, point to Picture, then click New Photo Album. The Photo Album dialog box lets you select the pictures, specify color values and brightness, choose whether you want black and white pictures, select a shape for the frame, and decide whether or not to rotate the images. You can apply any of the available design templates. You select the picture layout, which can either fit the pictures to the slide, or place as many pictures as you like on each slide. You put the selected pictures in the order you need for the album, decide if you want captions below the pictures, and then click Create. The photo album is created as a presentation you can then modify.

Figure 3-8: Fill effects dialog box

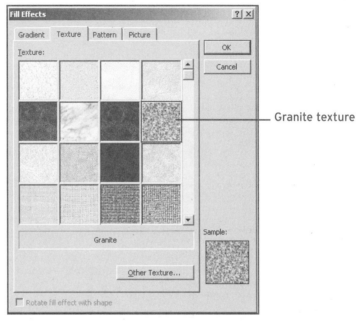

Granite texture

Figure 3-9: Granite texture applied to background

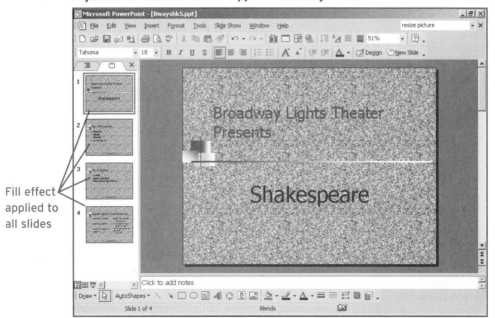

Fill effect
applied to
all slides

Skill Set 3
Inserting and Modifying Visual Elements

Customize Slide Backgrounds
Add Bitmap Graphics to Slide Backgrounds

You might have a particular image such as a logo that you want to feature prominently in your presentation. You can use any image as the background for all or some of the slides in the presentation. You can select a photograph that you created with a digital camera, an image that you made using graphics editing software, or any image stored as a file on your computer. You use the Picture tab of the Fill Effects dialog box to select a picture as a background image.

Activity Steps

 open Bwayshk6.ppt

1. Click **Slide 3**, click **Format** on the menu bar, then click **Background**

2. Click the **Background fill list arrow**, click **Fill Effects**, then click the **Picture tab** in the Fill Effects dialog box

3. Click **Select Picture**, navigate to the folder where your Project Files are stored, click **flower1.jpg** in the Select Picture dialog box, then click **Insert**
See Figure 3-10.

4. Click **OK**, then click **Apply**
You often have to modify text to accommodate the characteristics of the image you selected for a background. This picture has a dark spot where the slide title text is currently placed.

5. Click **Old Favorites**, click the **Align Right button** on the toolbar, then click outside the slide to deselect it
See Figure 3-11.

 close Bwayshk6.ppt

Step 3
Click the Lock aspect ratio check box in the Fill Effects dialog box to prevent the image from becoming distorted when it is resized to fit the slide.

Figure 3-10: Fill Effects dialog box with flower1 selected

Figure 3-11: Graphic applied to slide background

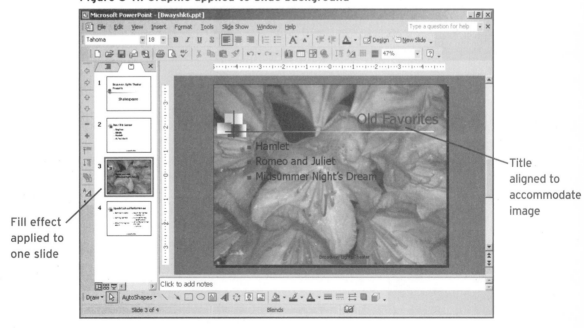

Fill effect applied to one slide

Title aligned to accommodate image

Skill Set 3
Inserting and Modifying Visual Elements

Add OfficeArt Elements to Slides
Add Freeform Objects and AutoShapes to Slides

You can use the various drawing tools available on the Drawing toolbar to create unique shapes and graphic elements to enhance your presentation. If you don't want to draw shapes yourself, you can choose from one of the many ready-made AutoShapes, also available on the Drawing toolbar. You can use the Drawing toolbar buttons to customize the shape with colors, line widths, and line styles to get the exact effect you want.

You can change the colors, line styles, position, and size of an AutoShape using the Format AutoShape dialog box. To open the Format AutoShape dialog box, double-click the AutoShape.

Activity Steps

 open Bwayshk7.ppt

1. Click **Slide 2**, click the **Oval button** on the Drawing toolbar, place the ┼ pointer slightly above the bullet next to **Comedy of Errors**, then drag down and right to create an oval around Comedy of Errors

2. Click the **Fill Color button list arrow** on the Drawing toolbar, click **No Fill**, then click the **Line Style button**

3. Point to the **3pt single line style** as shown in Figure 3-12, then click **3pt single line style**

4. Click the **Arrow button** on the Drawing toolbar, drag the ┼ pointer from the bottom middle sizing handle on the oval down and right to the middle of the two columns just below the last bullet

5. Click the **Line Style button**, click the **3pt single line style**, click the **Arrow Style button** on the Drawing toolbar, then click **Arrow Style 6** (the left facing arrow)

6. Click **AutoShapes** on the Drawing toolbar, point to **Stars and Banners**, then click **Vertical Scroll** (column 1 row 4)

7. Drag the ┼ pointer from the beginning of the arrow down and right to create a scroll 2½" wide and 1" tall, then type **Special Holiday Performance**
   See Figure 3-13.

 close Bwayshk7.ppt

Figure 3-12: Drawing an oval

Oval drawn on slide

Fill Color list arrow

Oval button

Current line width

New line width

Line Style button

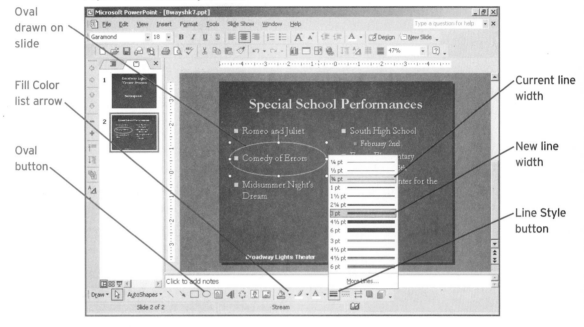

Figure 3-13: Slide with Autoshape and freeform objects

Arrow

Arrow button

AutoShape

Arrow Style button

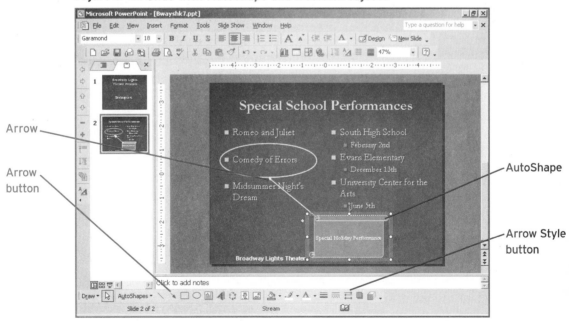

Skill Set 3
Inserting and Modifying Visual Elements

Add OfficeArt Elements to Slides
Add an Organization Chart to a Slide

Although you could use the drawing tools to create conceptual drawings, PowerPoint's diagramming tools let you create certain types of diagrams quickly. **Organization charts**, often called **org charts**, combine text and graphics to create a representation of how people or things are related to each other. They are often used to show the hierarchy of employees in a business. In an organization chart, shapes are connected by lines to show relationships. Items at a higher level in the hierarchy are known as **superior** shapes and feed into lesser items such as **assistant** shapes, **subordinate** shapes, and **coworker** shapes. Typically the most important item is at the top, although you can invert the chart. To insert an organization chart, you use the Insert Diagram or Organization Chart button, which is located on both the Drawing toolbar and the Content slide layout. The Organization Chart toolbar has buttons that let you change the chart layout, expand, scale, or fit the contents to the chart, and insert new subordinates, coworkers, or assistants.

Activity Steps

 open Bwayshk8.ppt

1. Click **Slide 2**, click **View** on the menu bar, click **Task Pane**, click the **Other Task Panes** down arrow, click **Slide Layout**, then click the **Title and Content layout** in the Content Layouts area

2. Click the **Insert Diagram or Organization Chart button** on the Content Layout template placeholder, click the **Organization Chart diagram type** in the Diagram Gallery, then click **OK**
See Figure 3-14.

Right-click a shape to open a shortcut menu with commands to help you create organization charts.

3. Click the **top shape**, click the **Font Color list arrow**, click **More Colors**, click the **Black cell**, click **OK**, type **Jennifer Laina**, press **[Enter]**, type **Producer**, then press **[Esc]**

4. Click the **left subordinate shape**, click the black **Font Color button**, type **Emily Michaels**, press **[Enter]**, type **Director**, then press **[Esc]**

5. Click the **middle shape**, click the black **Font Color button**, type **Rita Backer**, press **[Enter]**, type **Staging**, then press **[Esc]**

6. Click the **right shape**, click the black **Font Color button**, type **Karen Louie**, press **[Enter]**, type **Casting**, then press **[Esc]**

7. Click outside the chart to deselect it, then close the task pane
See Figure 3-15.

close Bwayshk8.ppt

Figure 3-14: Organization chart on slide

Organization chart

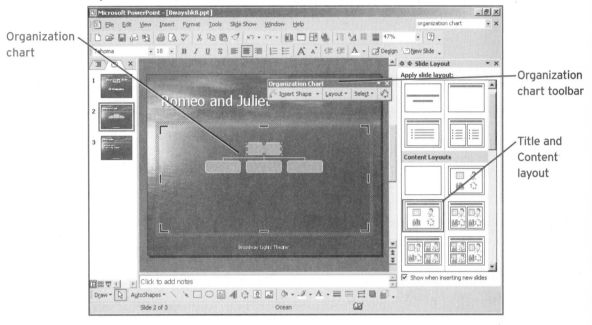

Organization chart toolbar

Title and Content layout

Figure 3-15: Completed organization chart

Subordinate shapes

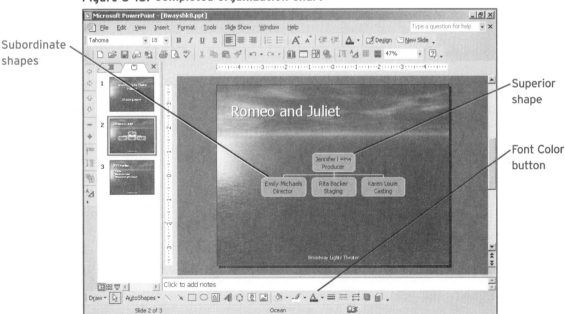

Superior shape

Font Color button

Skill Set 3
Inserting and Modifying Visual Elements

Apply Custom Formats to Tables
Apply User-Defined Formats to Tables

Tables organize information so that it is easier for an audience to understand. Formatting tables makes data even more visually comprehensible. For instance, applying different colors to each row or to column heads can help distinguish them from other elements of the table. Applying a decorative line style to your borders can also make your table more appealing. These and other formatting commands are available on the Tables and Borders toolbar and the Format menu.

Activity Steps

 open Bwayshk9.ppt

1. Click **Slide 2**, click the table to select it, then open the Tables and Borders toolbar

2. Drag the pointer to select the **Afternoon row**, click the **Center Vertically button** on the Tables and Borders toolbar, click the **Fill Color list arrow** , then click the **Pink custom color square** in the second row of the palette

3. Drag to select the **Evening row**, click the **Center Vertically button** , click the **Fill Color list arrow** , then click **More Fill Colors**

4. Click the **Custom tab**, type **130** in the Red box, press **[Tab]**, type **56** in the Green box, press **[Tab]**, type **250** in the Blue box, click **OK**, then click in the first cell
See Figure 3-16.

5. Double-click the **table border** to open the Format Table dialog box, scroll the **Borders Style list**, click the **long dash, dot line style** (the last one in the list), click the **three horizontal border buttons** off and then on again (top, middle, and bottom) to apply the new dashed border to all horizontal borders, then click **OK**

6. Drag the pointer to select the **Child**, **Student**, and **Adult cells**, then click the **Bold button** on the toolbar

7. Click **cell 1**, click **Format** on the menu bar, click **Table**, click the **Fill tab**, click the **Fill color list arrow**, click **Fill Effects**, click the **Two colors option button**, click the **Color 1 list arrow**, click the **Pink color square** on the second row, click the **Color 2 list arrow**, click the **Blue color square** on the second row, click **OK**, click **OK** again, then click to deselect the table
See Figure 3-17.

 close Bwayshk9.ppt

Step 4
To get exact colors, you can enter the exact values. This is useful if you are trying to match colors.

Figure 3-16: Changing table formats

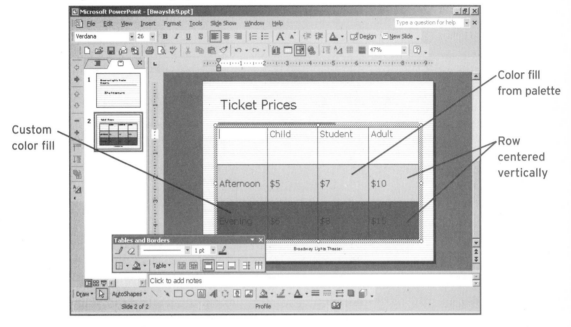

Figure 3-17: Final formatted table

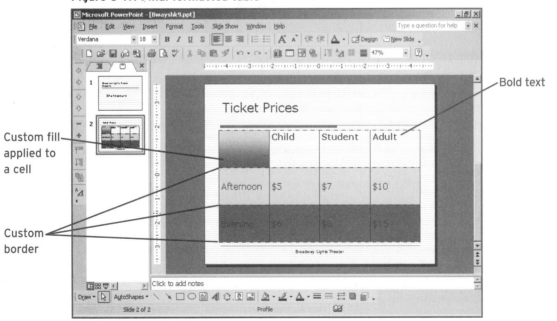

Skill Set 3

Inserting and Modifying Visual Elements

Target Your Skills

 open Pretzel1.ppt

1 Use Figure 3-18 to finish a presentation for the PerfectPretzel company. The column headings in the table are PA, CT, NJ, NY. The row labels are Manager and Assistant Manager.

Figure 3-18

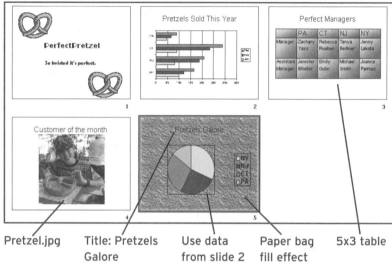

Pretzel.jpg   Title: Pretzels Galore   Use data from slide 2   Paper bag fill effect   5x3 table

 open cat1.ppt

2 Use Figure 3-19 as a guide to create a final presentation. Add an organization chart to slide 2 showing you as the Director and the four shelters as subordinate shapes. Click the Insert Shape button on the Organization Chart toolbar to insert a coworker.

Figure 3-19

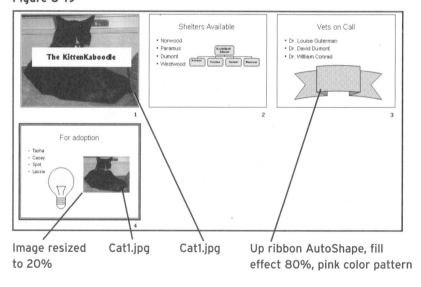

Image resized to 20%   Cat1.jpg   Cat1.jpg   Up ribbon AutoShape, fill effect 80%, pink color pattern

Skill List

1. Apply formats to presentations
2. Apply animation schemes
3. Apply slide transitions
4. Customize slide formats
5. Customize slide templates
6. Manage a Slide Master
7. Rehearse timing
8. Rearrange slides
9. Modify slide layout
10. Add links to a presentation

PowerPoint comes with a wide variety of tools to help you control and format your presentations. In this skill set, you'll learn how to make formatting changes to design templates, slide masters, and slide layouts to enhance your presentations. You'll also learn to add and customize color and animation schemes and apply transition effects for an entire presentation or individual slides. To help you prepare for a live audience, you'll also rehearse and change the timings for your presentation and rearrange slides as needed. Finally, you'll add hyperlinks to other slides within the presentation, other files on your computer, an intranet, or the Web.

Skill Set 4
Modifying Presentation Formats

Apply Formats to Presentations
Format Slides Differently in a Single Presentation

You do not have to be a graphic designer to create professional-looking presentations. You can apply any of the design templates that come with PowerPoint to some or all of your slides to take advantage of great-looking layouts, graphics, and colors that work well together. The Slide Design task pane contains all the available design templates. Once you apply a particular design template, you can easily make modifications to individual slides to create a unique look for background graphics, bullets, text, and color.

Use the Bullets and Numbering dialog box to change the bullet color, the numbering style, or the size of the bullet relative to the text. To use a picture as a bullet, click Picture, choose an available image or click Import to browse for one, then click OK.

Activity Steps

 open Hamlet1.ppt

1. Click the **Design button** to open the Slide Design task pane, then click **Slide 4** on the Slides tab

2. Scroll the Slide Design task pane to view the Available For Use design templates, then click the **Digital Dots template icon**
   See Figure 4-1.

3. Click the **left text box** on the slide, press and hold **[Shift]**, then click the **right text box** to select both text boxes

4. Click **Format** on the menu bar, click **Bullets and Numbering**, verify that the **Bulleted tab** is selected, click the **four dots in a diamond pattern** bullet design, then click **OK**

5. Click the **Font Size list arrow** on the toolbar, then click **28**

6. Close the Slide Design task pane, click **Slide 3** on the Slides tab to view the original formatting of the design template, then click **Slide 4** on the Slides tab to view the formatting modifications you made
   See Figure 4-2.

 close Hamlet1.ppt

Figure 4-1: Design template applied

Digital Dots applied

Slide 4 is selected

Digital Dots template

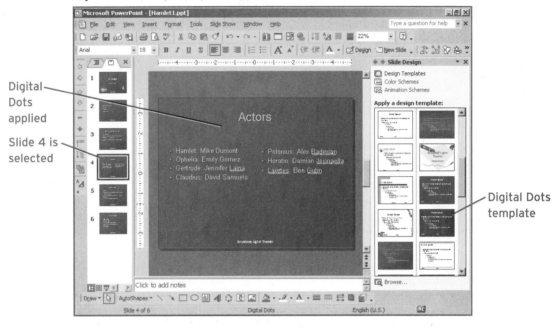

Figure 4-2: Formatting changes to slide

Font size changed for this slide

Bullet format changed for this slide

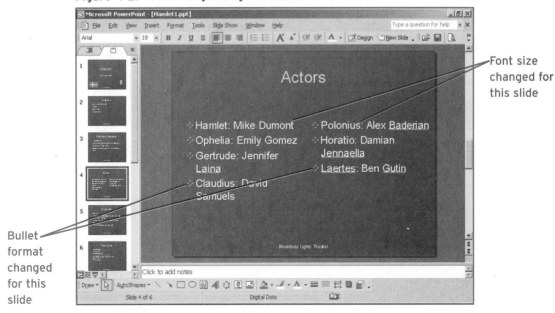

Skill Set 4
Modifying Presentation Formats

Apply Formats to Presentations
Modify Presentation Templates

Design templates contain text and bullet styles, background images, and color schemes that give your presentation a professional look. However, you might want to make formatting modifications to one or more of these elements to create a design that better meets the needs of your presentation. All the specifications for a design template are stored in the slide master, the part of the presentation that specifies how graphics and text appear on each slide. Formatting changes made to text, bullets, and other elements in the slide master will be applied to every slide in the presentation.

Activity Steps

 open Hamlet2.ppt

1. Click **Slide 5** on the Slides tab, click **View**, point to **Master**, then click **Slide Master**
   See Figure 4-3.

You can also open the slide master by pressing and holding [Shift], then clicking the Normal View button.

2. Click **Click to edit Master title style**, click the **Font Style list arrow**, then click **Algerian**, or another font if Algerian is not available

3. Right-click **Click to edit Master text styles**, click **Bullets and Numbering** on the shortcut menu, click **Customize**, type **150** in the Character code box to select the symbol **Wingdings 150**, click **OK**, then click **OK** again (Note: If you do not have the Wingdings 150 symbol, click another symbol)

4. Click the **Normal View button**

5. Click the **Slide Sorter View button** , click the **Zoom list arrow** on the toolbar, then click **100%** to see the changes applied to all the slides
   See Figure 4-4.

 close Hamlet2.ppt

Figure 4-3: Slide Master view

Slide Master
View toolbar

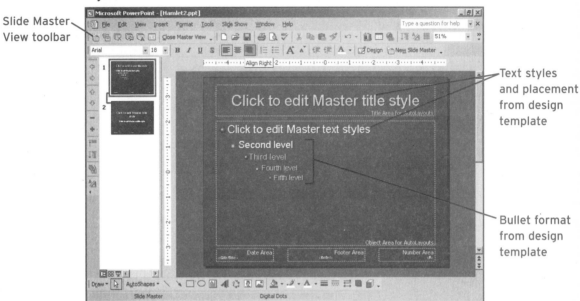

Text styles
and placement
from design
template

Bullet format
from design
template

Figure 4-4: Slide Sorter view

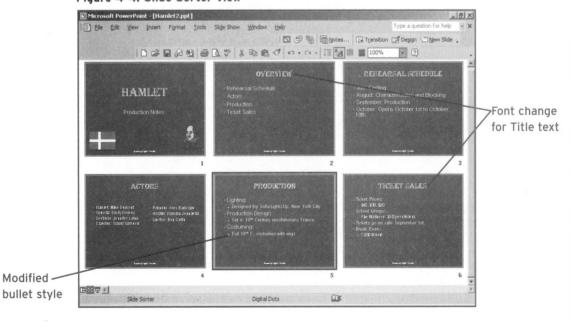

Font change
for Title text

Modified
bullet style

Skill Set 4
Modifying Presentation Formats

Apply Formats to Presentations
Modify the Format of Individual Slides

Choosing a design template applies set colors, fonts, and bullet styles to your presentation. Sometimes, you might want to make a change to an individual slide so that it is formatted differently from the rest of the slides in your presentation. For instance, you might want to change the color scheme for one slide so that it stands out from the rest. A **color scheme** is a set of eight colors that is consistently applied to fonts, accents, hyperlinks, backgrounds, and fills. PowerPoint comes with several color schemes that you can apply to all or selected slides. Each design template has a set color scheme that you can change for individual slides or the entire presentation, as needed. Changing the color scheme can alter the whole feel of a presentation; use the Slide Design task pane to change the color scheme.

Activity Steps

 open Hamlet3.ppt

tip

You can override the slide master formatting for individual slides by using the Format menu.

1. Click the **Design button** on the toolbar to open the Slide Design task pane, then click **Color Schemes**
   The selected color scheme is currently applied to the entire presentation.

2. Click **Slide 3** on the Slides tab, press and hold **[Shift]**, then click **Slide 6** on the Slide tab
   See Figure 4-5.

3. Click the **teal background color scheme list arrow** (the fourth color scheme in the first column), then click **Apply to Selected Slides**
   See Figure 4-6.

 close Hamlet3.ppt

Figure 4-5: Default color scheme applied to all slides

Modify the format of these selected slides

Color scheme currently applied

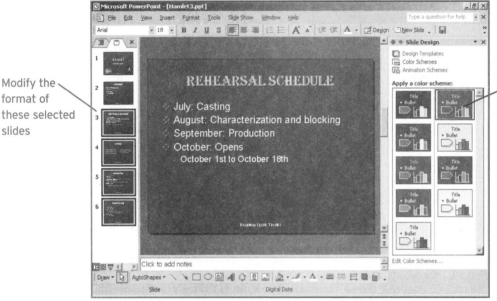

Figure 4-6: New color scheme applied to selected slides

Color scheme applied to selected slides

Color scheme list arrow

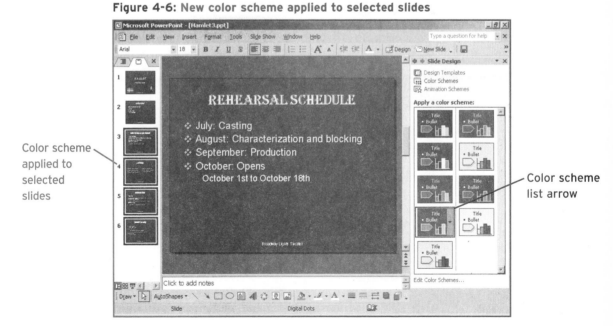

Skill Set 4

Modifying Presentation Formats

Apply Formats to Presentations
Apply More than One Design Template to Presentations

Design templates come with default color schemes as well as graphics, bullet, and font styles. You can enhance any presentation by applying more than one design template to it. When you apply a new design template to selected slides, the graphics and specifications for color and text are copied from the slide master in the new design template to a corresponding slide master for those selected slides. You can have more than one slide master in a presentation. Most design templates have slide master pairs: one master for the title slide and another for all other slides. To apply a new design template, use the Slide Design task pane.

Activity Steps

 open Hamlet4.ppt

1. Click **Slide 2** in the Slides tab, press and hold **[Ctrl]**, click **Slide 4**, press and hold **[Ctrl]**, then click **Slide 6**
   Slides 2, 4, and 6 are selected.

2. Click the **Design button** on the toolbar to open the Slide Design task pane, then click **Design Templates** to display all available design templates

Not all design templates contain both a slide master and title master. To add a title master, click Insert on the menu bar, then click New Title Master.

3. Scroll the list of templates, click the **Digital Dots.pot template list arrow**, then click **Apply to Selected Slides**

4. Scroll to the top of the Apply a design template list, then place the pointer on the **Digital Dots** template in the Used in This Presentation section to display the screen tip
   See Figure 4-7.

5. Click **View** on the menu bar, point to **Master**, then click **Slide Master**
   The presentation now contains two slide master pairs; each pair consists of a slide master for the title slide and a slide master for all other slides.

6. Close the Slide Design task pane
   See Figure 4-8.

 close Hamlet4.ppt

Figure 4-7: Digital Dots design template applied to selected slides

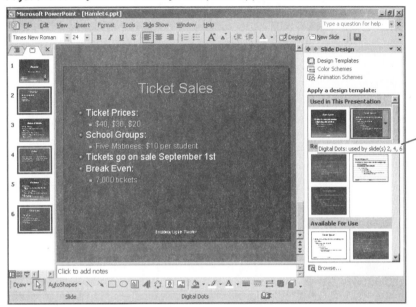

ScreenTip tells you which slides use the design template

Figure 4-8: Presentation with two slide master pairs

Original slide master and title master pair

Second slide master and title master added when Digital Dots template was applied to selected slides

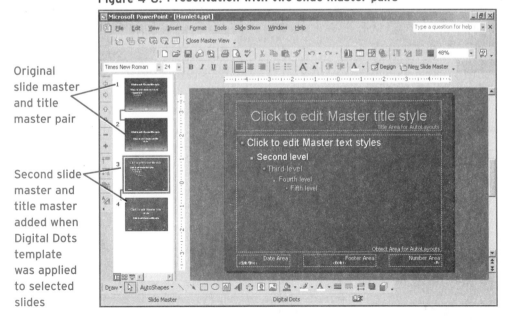

Skill Set 4
Modifying Presentation Formats

Apply Animation Schemes
Apply an Animation Scheme to a Single Slide

Animation is the motion of text and objects on a slide along with special visual and sound effects. You can bring life to your presentations by using animation. PowerPoint comes with an astounding array of ways to make text and graphics spin, swirl, and interact. You can choose from professionally designed **animation schemes**, which apply preset visual effects to text on a slide. Animation schemes are available in the Slide Design task pane, divided into three categories: Subtle, Moderate, and Exciting, to help you choose just the right animation for your presentation and audience. You can also apply preset **transitions** to your slides, which are effects that take the presentation from one slide to the next. Some animation schemes also include transitions. If both animation and transition effects are applied to a slide, transition effects occur first.

Select No Animation in the Slide Design task pane to remove animation from a slide.

Activity Steps

 open Hamlet5.ppt

1. Click the **Design button** on the toolbar to open the Slide Design task pane

2. Click **Animation Schemes**

3. Click **Slide 4** on the Slides tab

4. Scroll through the list of subtle animation schemes, scroll through the list of Moderate animation schemes, then click **Credits** in the Exciting animation scheme list
   See Figure 4-9.

5. Click the **Slide Show (from current slide) button** 🖳 to view the animation

 close Hamlet5.ppt

Figure 4-9: Apply an animation scheme to one slide

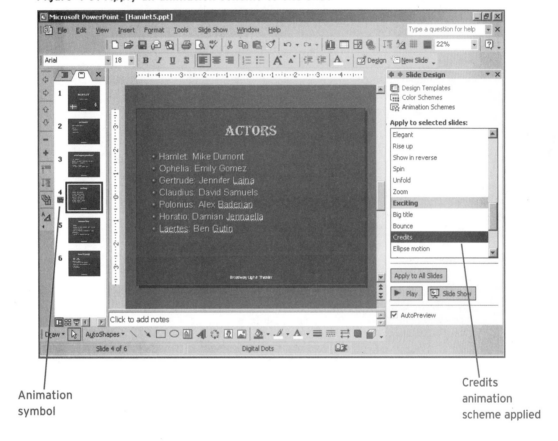

Animation symbol

Credits animation scheme applied

extra!

Viewing the slide show

The best way to get a sense of how the presentation is going to look with the animations you've chosen is by viewing the slide show during development. You can do this by clicking the slide from which you want to start and then clicking the Slide Show button on the Slide Design task pane or the Slide Show (from current slide) button. You can also view the show by clicking View on the menu bar, then clicking Slide Show, or by pressing [F5] at any time from any view. To stop the show at any time, press [Esc].

Skill Set 4
Modifying Presentation Formats

Apply Animation Schemes
Apply an Animation Scheme to a Group of Slides

You can apply animation schemes to a selected group of slides by selecting the slides you want and choosing an animation scheme from the Slide Design task pane. Animation schemes can include any combination of transition effects or title and body animations. If you want to animate only certain elements on your slide, you can use the Custom Animation task pane to select those elements and then choose a type of animation to apply to them. You should be careful as you apply animation schemes in a presentation; while selective use of animations can focus attention on a particular point, too much animation can detract from your message.

tip

To select contiguous slides, click the first slide, press and hold [Shift] then click the last slide.

Activity Steps

 open Hamlet6.ppt

1. Click the **Design button** 🔲 on the toolbar to open the Slide Design task pane

2. Click **Slide 2** on the Slides tab, press and hold **[Ctrl]**, click **Slide 3**, press and hold **[Ctrl]**, click **Slide 5**, press and hold **[Ctrl]**, then click **Slide 6**
   See Figure 4-10.

3. Scroll through the list of subtle animation schemes, scroll through the list of Moderate animation schemes, then click **Pinwheel** in the Exciting animation scheme list

4. Click the **Slide Sorter View button** 🔲
   See Figure 4-11.

5. Click **Slide 1**, then click the **Slide Show (from current slide) button** 🖥 to view the show

    close Hamlet6.ppt

---

extra!

Creating Custom Animations
You can animate individual elements of a slide using the Custom Animation task pane. Click Slide Show on the menu bar, then click Custom Animation to open the Custom Animation task pane. To animate individual elements, select the element, click Add Effect in the task pane, then choose an animation style from the menu. You can also modify the start, property, and speed effects for each animation that you apply. You can also change the order in which text appears by clicking the Reorder arrows.

Figure 4-10: Apply an animation scheme to a group of slides

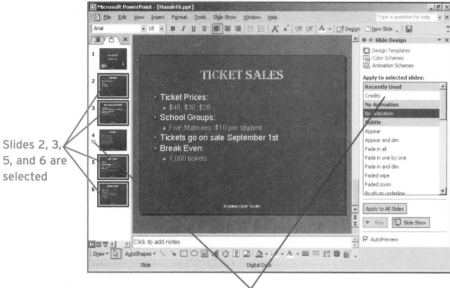

Slides 2, 3, 5, and 6 are selected

Credits animation scheme was recently used and applied to slide 4

Figure 4-11: Slide Sorter view showing animations

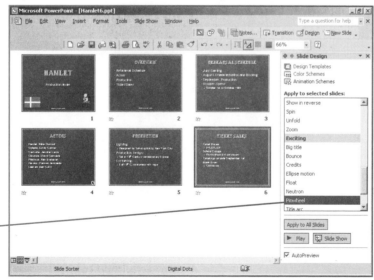

Pinwheel animation applied to slides 2, 3, 5, and 6

Skill Set 4

Modifying Presentation Formats

Apply Animation Schemes
Apply an Animation Scheme to an Entire Presentation

If you want the animations in your slides to have a consistent appearance, you can apply a single animation scheme to the entire presentation. If your presentation already contains several animation schemes, you can override the current schemes by applying a new scheme to the entire presentation.

Text or an object must have an animation applied to it before you can add a custom animation.

Activity Steps

 open Hamlet7.ppt

1. Click the **Normal View button**, Click **Slide 1** on the Slides tab, then click the **Slide Show (from current slide) button**

2. Press [PgDn] as many times as necessary to view the entire show and return to Normal view

3. Click the **Design button** to open the Slide Design task pane, click **Animation Schemes**, then click **Wipe** in the Subtle list

4. Click **Apply to All Slides** in the Slide Design task pane
   See Figure 4-12.

5. Click the **Slide Show (from current slide) button**, then press [Enter] as needed to view all slides with the new animation scheme

 close Hamlet7.ppt

Figure 4-12: Apply an animation scheme to all slides in a show

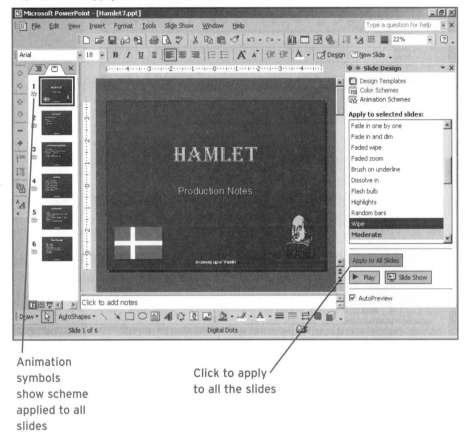

Animation symbols show scheme applied to all slides

Click to apply to all the slides

extra!

Understanding animation categories

PowerPoint organizes animation schemes into three categories in the Slide Design task pane: subtle, moderate, and exciting. Although somewhat subjective, these categories will help you choose the most appropriate animation for your presentation. In the Custom Animation task pane, animation effects are divided into four categories: Entrance (determines how text or object enters the slide), Emphasis (adds an effect to an object that is already on the slide), Exit (determines how the text or object leaves the slide at some point while the slide is displayed on the screen), and Motion paths (the path the object takes on a slide as part of the animation). You should view the effects before deciding which ones you will use. If you plan to use several effects in a show, you might want to select from the same group to keep the feel of the effects consistent.

Skill Set 4

Modifying Presentation Formats

Apply Slide Transitions
Apply Transition Effects to a Single Slide

The **transition** between slides occurs when the previous slide leaves the screen and a new slide appears. PowerPoint offers several **transition effects** you can use to liven up transitions. To apply a transition effect to selected slides, you use the Slide Transition task pane. Though you can apply only one transition effect to each slide, you can adjust the timing and the trigger for each effect. Transition effects may or may not be included in an animation scheme. You can add or change transition effects from any view.

A star symbol under a slide in Slide Sorter view, or under the slide number in the Slides tab, indicates that a transition effect or animation has been applied to the slide. Click the symbol to preview the transition or animation.

Activity Steps

 open Hamlet8.ppt

1. Click **Slide 3** on the Slides tab

2. Click **Slide Show** on the menu bar, then click **Slide Transition** to open the Slide Transition task pane
   See Figure 4-13.

3. Scroll the list of transitions, then click **Newsflash**

4. Click the **Speed list arrow** in the Modify transition section, then click **Slow**
   See Figure 4-14.

5. Click the **Slide Show button** in the Slide Transition task pane to view the show

 close Hamlet8.ppt

Figure 4-13: Slide Transition task pane

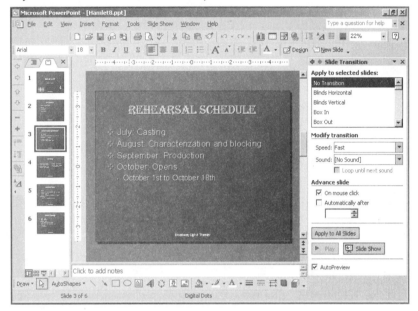

Figure 4-14: Newsflash transition

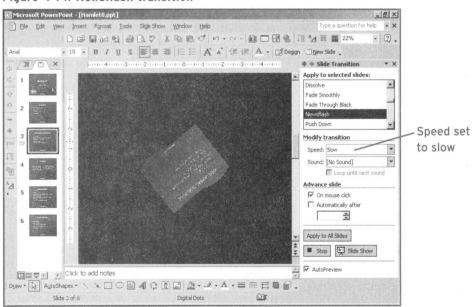

Speed set to slow

Skill Set 4

Modifying Presentation Formats

Apply Slide Transitions
Apply Transition Effects to a Group of Slides in a Presentation

To keep a presentation interesting, you might want to apply one transition to some of the slides and a different transition to others. Content may drive your decision. For example, a slide with important figures or facts can make a bold statement if you apply the Cut Through Black transition. Somber news can be introduced with a slow Dissolve transition. Adding sound such as a drum roll can highlight a specific slide. You can add or edit transition effects from Normal or Slide Sorter view using the Slide Transition task pane.

Many transition effects have descriptive names that tell you which direction they will progress, such as Wipe Left or Checkerboard Down. To change the direction of a transition effect, choose the appropriately named transition from the Slide Transition task pane.

Activity Steps

 open Hamlet9.ppt

1. Click the **Zoom list arrow**, then click **50%** to see all the slides in Slide Sorter view

2. Click **Slide 1**, press and hold **[Ctrl]**, click **Slide 4**, press and hold **[Ctrl]**, then click **Slide 6**

3. Click the **Transition button** [🔲], scroll through the Slide Transition task pane, click **Wheel Clockwise, 3 spokes** in the Slide Transition task pane
   See Figure 4-15.

4. Click **Slide 1**, click **Slide show** in the task pane, then press **[Enter]** as needed to view the entire show

 close Hamlet9.ppt

Figure 4-15: Transition applied to selected slides

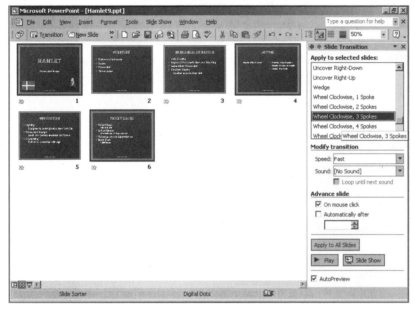

extra!

Specifying how to advance slides

The Slide Transition task pane offers options for how to advance from one slide to the next in a slide show. The On mouse click option makes it necessary for the presenter to click or press [Enter], [Tab], or [PgDn] to advance to the next slide. To make the show run without intervention, click the Automatically after check box, then specify a time interval in the box.

Skill Set 4
Modifying Presentation Formats

Apply Slide Transitions
Apply Transition Effects to an Entire Presentation

To keep a presentation professional-looking and cohesive, you might want to apply one transition to all the slides. You can do this from either Normal or Slide Sorter view, using the Slide Transition task pane.

Click the Play button in the Slide Transition task pane to view the transition effects in the selected slides.

Activity Steps

 open Hamlet10.ppt

1. Click the **Transition button** on the toolbar to open the Slide Transition task pane

2. Click **Fade Through Black** in the Slide Transition task pane

3. Click **Apply to All Slides**
   See Figure 4-16.

4. Click **Slide Show** in the task pane, then press **[Enter]** as needed to view the entire presentation

 close Hamlet10.ppt

Figure 4-16: Transition effect applied to all the slides

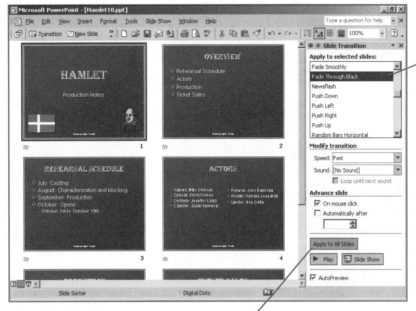

Fade Through Black transition effect

Click to apply transition to all slides

Skill Set 4

Modifying Presentation Formats

Customize Slide Formats
Customize Slides

A design template provides unique formatting specifications for text, bullets, graphics, and color that you can apply to any or all slides in a presentation. Every design template has a set **color scheme**, which is a group of specified colors applied consistently to the background, titles, fills, and bullets on slides. When you apply a design template to selected slides, all the formatting specifications for that design template are applied to the slide master. However, if you want certain slides to stand out from the others, you can override the design template formatting specified by the slide master. For instance, you can modify any of the elements of a color scheme and apply the revised color scheme to selected slides. Any edited color schemes will be available to you as new color schemes in the Slide Design task pane. The custom color schemes you create do not change the slide master formatting or color scheme for the rest of the slides in the presentation, and if you add a new slide it will take on the characteristics of the slide master.

If you inadvertently apply any color scheme to all the slides by mistake, click Edit on the menu bar, then click Undo.

Activity Steps

 open Bitpress1.ppt

1. Click the **Design button** on the toolbar, then click **Slide 3** on the Slides tab

2. Click **Color Schemes** in the task pane
   The selected color scheme determined by the Crayons design template specifies a red title, small square bullet, black text, and yellow fill.

3. Click the **purple background color scheme list arrow** (first column fourth scheme), then click **Apply to Selected Slides**
   See Figure 4-17.

4. Click **Edit Color Schemes** in the Slide Design task pane, click the **Standard tab**, click the **purple background color scheme** (third row first scheme), then click the **Custom tab**

5. Click the **Title text white color box**, click **Change Color**, click the **Bright yellow color box** as shown in Figure 4-18, then click **OK**

6. Click **Apply** to close the Edit Color Scheme text box
   The edited color scheme appears as a new option in the Apply a color scheme list.

7. Click **Slide 4** in the Slides tab, click the new **yellow title with purple background** color scheme list arrow (first column fifth scheme), then click **Apply to Selected Slides**

 close bitpress1.ppt

Figure 4-17: Slide Design task pane with color schemes displayed

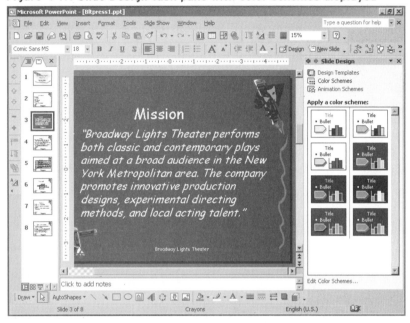

Figure 4-18: Creating a custom color scheme

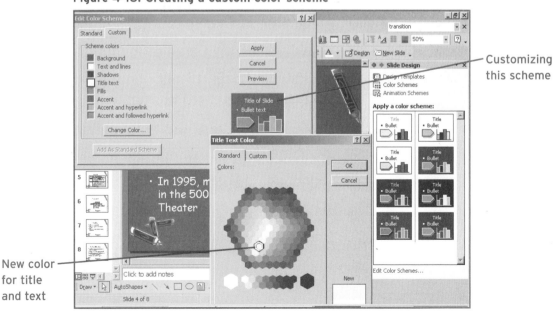

Customizing this scheme

New color for title and text

Skill Set 4
Modifying Presentation Formats

Customize Slide Templates
Customize Templates

Every design template includes formatting for placeholders that contain text, graphics, and other types of content. All of the formatting specifications for these placeholders and their content are contained in the slide master. If you want to make global changes to fonts, bullets, or placeholders throughout your presentation, you make these changes to the slide master in Slide Master view. Many design templates contain two slides in Slide Master view: the **Title Master**, which contains the layout and formatting specifications for the title slide, and the **Slide Master**, which contains specifications for all non-title slides. A slide master and title master are referred to as **slide master pairs**. Titles can have different alignments, margins, tabs, font sizes, and styles from the body text. If you modify the default settings in the slide master for a design template, you can save it as a new template to use in any new presentation.

Step 6
Click View on the menu bar then click Ruler to display or hide the ruler.

Activity Steps

 open Bitpress2.ppt

1. Click **View** on the menu bar, point to **Master**, then click **Slide Master**
   Slide 1 is the slide master; slide 2 is the title master.
2. Click **Slide 2** to select the title master, click **Click to edit Master subtitle style**, click the **Font Color list arrow** , then click the **blue box** (eighth box on the right)
3. Click **Slide 1**, click **Click to edit Master title style**, then click the **Shadow button** [S] on the toolbar
4. Click **Click to edit Master text styles** on the slide master, click **Format** on the menu bar, click **Bullets and Numbering**, click the **open square boxes**, click the **Color list arrow**, click the **red box**, then click **OK**
5. Right-click **Second level**, click **Bullets and Numbering**, click the **solid square boxes**, click the **Color list arrow**, click the **blue box**, then click **OK**
6. Drag the **leftmost margin marker** on the Horizontal Ruler 1/4" to the right on the ruler
   See Figure 4-19.
7. Click **File** on the menu bar, click **Save As**, click the **Save as type list arrow**, click **Design Template (*.pot)**, then type **Bitpress2-2** in the File name box
   See Figure 4-20.

8. Click **Save**

 close Bitpress2.ppt

Figure 4-19: Changes to slide masters

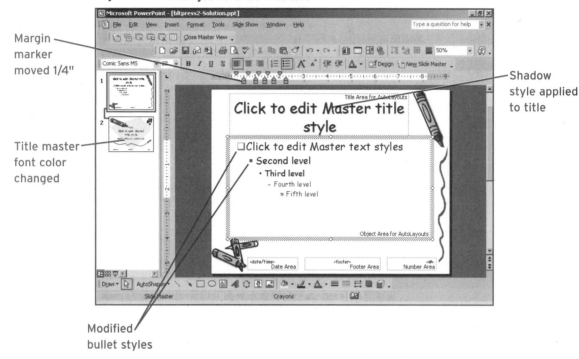

Margin marker moved 1/4"

Shadow style applied to title

Title master font color changed

Modified bullet styles

Figure 4-20: Saving a presentation as a design template

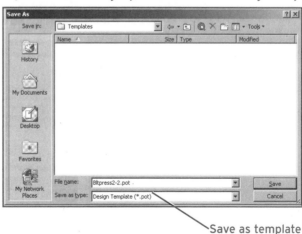

Save as template

Skill Set 4
Modifying Presentation Formats

Manage a Slide Master
Create and Manage a Slide Master

Global formatting changes to all the slides in your presentation are made to the slide master, the part of the presentation that specifies how text and graphics appear on each slide. You can use Slide Master view to change the arrangement of text placeholders or objects on the slide master, or make changes to font and bullet styles. Most design templates have two slide masters, known as a master pair; one master for the title slide and another for all other slides. You can have more than one master pair in any presentation. To insert a new slide master that uses PowerPoint default styles, click the Insert New Slide Master button on the Master View toolbar or begin a new blank presentation. To insert a new title master, click the Insert New Title Master button on the Slide Master View toolbar. To help manage slide masters, you can rename them by clicking the Rename Master button. If the presentation no longer uses a master, you can click the Delete Master button to delete both the slide master and title master.

The Master toolbar may be docked on the top, bottom, left, or right side of the window.

Activity Steps

1. Click the **New button** on the toolbar, click **View** on the menu bar, point to **Master**, then click **Slide Master**

2. Click **Click to edit Master title style**, click the **Underline button** on the toolbar, then click to deselect the text

3. Click the **Insert New Title Master button** on the toolbar, click the **Click to edit Master title style** placeholder on the new Title Master, then drag the placeholder up so the top of the box is at the 3" mark on the vertical ruler
   See Figure 4-21.

4. Click the **Rename Master button** on the toolbar, type **Underlined titles** in the Rename Master text box, click **Rename**, then click the **Normal View button**

5. Click **Click to add title**, type **American Pride**, click **Click to add subtitle**, type **Summer Meeting**, then click to deselect the placeholder
   See Figure 4-22.

 close the presentation

Figure 4-21: New slide title master with formatting changes

Slide Master
View toolbar

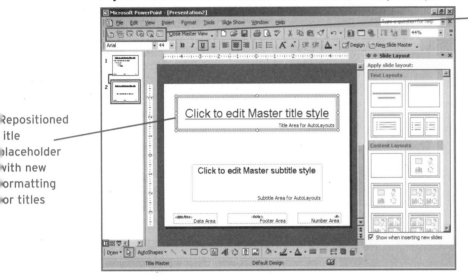

Repositioned
title
placeholder
with new
formatting
for titles

Figure 4-22: Using the new slide master

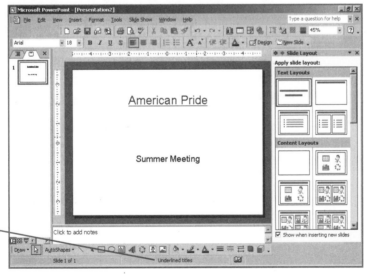

New slide
master is
applied

extra!

Restoring a layout

To restore a slide to its
original formatting,
click the Normal View
button, click Format on
the menu bar, click
Slide Layout, locate the
original layout from
the task pane, click that
layout list arrow, then
click Reapply Layout.

Skill Set 4

Modifying Presentation Formats

Manage a Slide Master
Create and Manage Multiple Slide Masters

In PowerPoint 2002, a presentation can have more than one slide master. Applying a new slide master to different slides lets you add variety to your presentation while maintaining a consistent design for groups of slides. If for some reason you want to limit the number of masters to one per presentation, you can disable this feature by clicking the Multiple masters check box on the Edit tab in the Options dialog box. You can also choose to **preserve** a master, which keeps it from being deleted if no slides use it in the presentation. To preserve a master, click the Preserve Master button on the Slide Master toolbar. A pushpin icon next to a master indicates it is preserved.

Activity Steps

 open Bitpress3.ppt

1. Click **View** on the menu bar, point to **Master**, then click **Slide Master**

2. Click the **Insert New Slide Master button** on the toolbar, click **Format** on the menu bar, click **Background**, click the **Color list arrow**, click the **first blue square in the second row**, then click **Apply**
   The new master has a preserved icon next to it; new masters are preserved by default.

3. Click the **Design button** on the toolbar, then click the **Profile.dot** template in the Apply a design template task pane
   The presentation now contains three different masters, two of which are paired with title masters. *See Figure 4-23.*

4. Click the **Normal View button** , click **Slide 2** on the Slides tab, click the **Custom Design** Master design template list arrow in the Used in This Presentation section of the task pane, then click **Apply to Selected Slides**

5. Click **Slide 6** in the Slides tab, press and hold **[Shift]**, click **Slide 8** to select slides 6-8, click the **Profile design template list arrow**, then click **Apply to Selected Slides**
   See Figure 4-24.

   close Bitpress3.ppt

To delete a slide master that you no longer want in the presentation, select it in Slide Master View, then click the Delete Master button on the Slide Master View toolbar.

Figure 4-23: Presentation with three slide masters

Slide masters with Title master pairs

Preserved Slide master with background change

Crayons design template

Custom design template

Profile design template

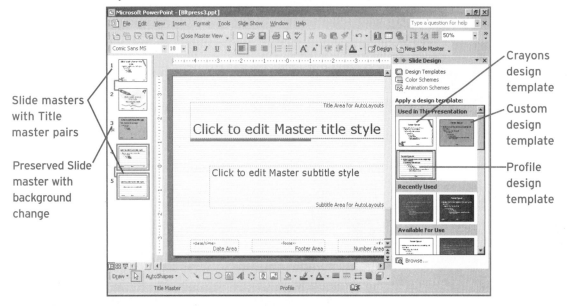

Figure 4-24: Slide masters applied to selected slides

Custom design template applied

Profile design template applied to slides 6, 7, 8

ScreenTip tells you which slides use the template

Crayons design template applied to slides 1, 3, 4, 5

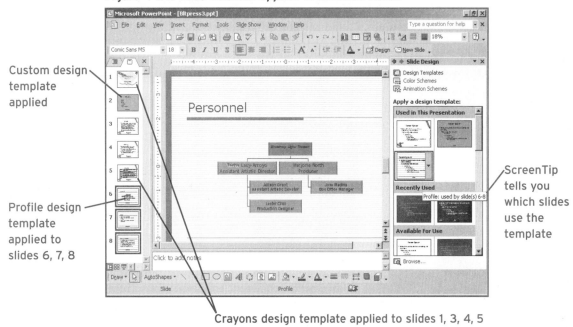

Skill Set 4
Modifying Presentation Formats

Rehearse Timing
Rehearse Presentations

If you are going to deliver your presentation to a live audience, you should be prepared. PowerPoint has many tools to help you rehearse your presentation. You can set the presentation to advance automatically from one slide to the next, or you can specify to advance manually by clicking the mouse or pressing a key on the keyboard. If you want your slides to advance automatically, you can specify the **Slide Timings** for the amount of time each slide appears on the screen in the Slide Transition task pane. You can specify the same or different timings for each or all the slides in the show. You can use the **Rehearse Timings** to help you determine the best amount of time to allot for each slide. To use this feature, click the Rehearse Timings button on the toolbar in Slide Sorter view, then set the timings for each slide on the Rehearse Timings bar that appears.

Activity Steps

 open Bitpress4.ppt

1. Click Slide 1 in Slide Sorter view, press and hold [Shift], click Slide 8, then click the Transition button on the toolbar to open the Slide Transition task pane
2. Scroll the list of transition effects in the Apply to selected slides box, click **Fade Through Black**, click the **Automatically after check box**, click the up arrow twice to specify **00:02**, then click the Slide pane
   See Figure 4-25.
3. Click Slide 1, click the Slide Show button in the Slide Transition task pane, view the show, then press any key to return to Slide Sorter view
   The Rehearse Timings button initiates a timer that begins counting immediately. You might want to read through step 4 and step 5 and then come back to complete the steps.
4. Click the Rehearse Timings button on the toolbar
   The first slide appears in Slide Show view, with the Rehearsal dialog box open in the upper left corner.
5. When the clock displays 12 seconds, click the Next button three times to advance to slide 2, then click the Rehearsal dialog box close button
6. Click Yes to keep the new slide timing for Slide 1 and return to Slide Sorter view
   See Figure 4-26. All the slides are set at 2 seconds except slide 1, which is set to 12 seconds.
7. Close the task pane

 close Bitpress4.ppt

tip

Click the Pause button on the Rehearsal toolbar while the timer is running if you need to take a break and want to save the timings.

Figure 4-25: Setting transition effects

Rehearse timings button

Fade Through Black transition

Timing set to advance automatically after 2 seconds for all slides

Click to watch the show

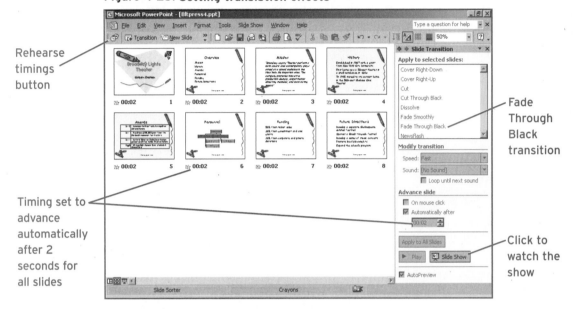

Figure 4-26: New timings after rehearsing the slide show

The new timing for slide 1

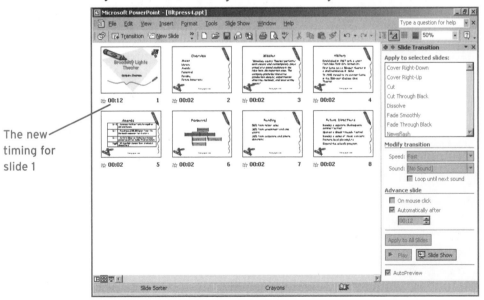

Skill Set 4
Modifying Presentation Formats

Rearrange Slides
Change the Order of Slides in Presentations

You can easily rearrange the order of slides in a presentation. You can work in Normal view using the Slides tab or in Slide Sorter view. To move a slide, drag it to the location you want. To create a copy of a slide and place it in a new location, press and hold [Ctrl] as you drag. You can also rearrange slides using the Outline tab by using the Move Up and Move Down buttons on the Outlining toolbar.

Activity Steps

 open Bitpress5.ppt

1. Click **Slide 3-Future Directions** in Slide Sorter view, then drag it to after Slide 8-Personnel

2. Click the **Normal View button** , click **View** on the menu bar, click **Normal (Restore panes),** click the **Outline tab** if it is not already displayed, then click the slide icon for Slide 6-Funding on the Outline tab
   See Figure 4-27.

3. Click the **Move Down button** on the Outline toolbar to move the Funding slide below the Personnel slide

4. Click the **Slides tab,** click **Slide 5-History** in the Slides tab, then drag it up using the pointer between slides 3 and 4

5. Click the **Slide Sorter View button**
   Compare your screen with Figure 4-28 to verify that the order is correct.

 close Bitpress5.ppt

Step 3
You can move slides in the Outline tab by dragging the Slide icon. A horizontal line shows the new placement on the tab as you move the slide.

Figure 4-27: Moving slides using the Outline tab

Move buttons on Outlining toolbar

Funding slide selected

Future Directions moved to slide 8

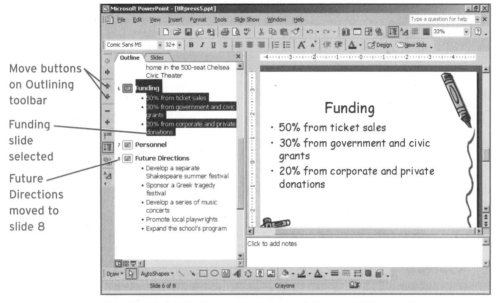

Figure 4-28: Final order after rearranging slides

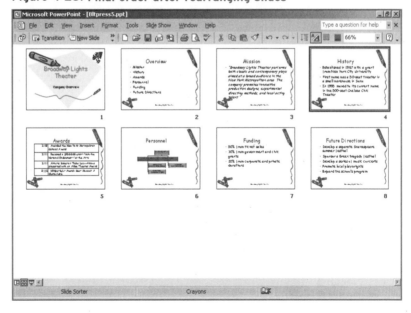

Skill Set 4

Modifying Presentation Formats

Modify Slide Layout
Change the Layout of Individual Slides

The Slide Layout task pane provides a wide array of layouts for different types of content. You may create a slide using one layout then decide another is more appropriate. You may determine that an image or chart is appropriate on a slide that currently only has text. Changing the layout does not affect the content but provides the new placeholders you need. Sometimes, though, you might want to make a formatting change to one of the sample layouts to accommodate the content for a particular slide. You can easily make changes to a layout by resizing or repositioning its placeholders or making another type of formatting change.

If you resize a text placeholder so that text no longer fits in it, the AutoFit Options button will appear next to the placeholder. Click this button to open its menu, then click AutoFit Text to Placeholder to resize the text automatically to fit.

Activity Steps

 open Hamlet11.ppt

1. Click **Format** on the menu bar, click **Slide Layout**, then click **Slide 2**

2. Click the **Title, Text, and Content layout** in the Text and Content Layouts section of the Slide Layout task pane as shown in Figure 4-29

3. Click **Slide 6** on the Slides tab, then click the **Title and 2-Column Text Layout** in the Text Layouts section of the Slide Layout task pane

4. Click **Click to add text**, type **Specials**, press **[Enter]**, then type **Seniors**

5. Click the Ticket Sales title placeholder, then use the ⬉ pointer to drag the lower-right sizing handle of the **Ticket Sales title placeholder** up and to the left to resize the placeholder so that the words appear on two lines and the first letters align with the words in the first bullet column
   See Figure 4-30.

 close Hamlet11.ppt

Figure 4-29: Changing the slide layout

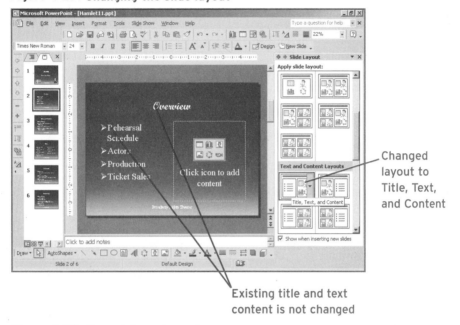

Changed
layout to
Title, Text,
and Content

Existing title and text
content is not changed

Figure 4-30: Reapplying a layout

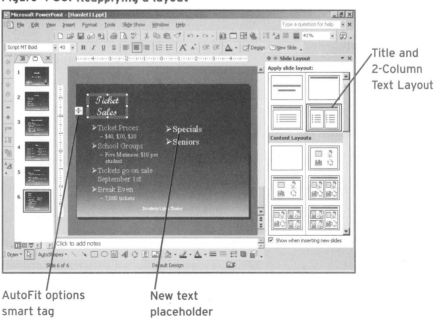

Title and
2-Column
Text Layout

AutoFit options
smart tag

New text
placeholder

Skill Set 4
Modifying Presentation Formats

Add Links to a Presentation
Add Hyperlinks to Slides

A **hyperlink** is text or an object on a slide that you click to connect to another location. In PowerPoint you can add hyperlinks on a slide to connect to another slide in the same presentation, a slide in another presentation, or a Web page on the Internet. A hyperlinked object can be a picture, graph, shape, or WordArt. If your hyperlink connects to another slide, the linked slide will display in PowerPoint. If your hyperlink connects to a Web page and your computer is connected to the Internet, the page will open in your default browser. You insert a hyperlink using the Insert Hyperlink button on the Standard toolbar.

Activity Steps

 open Hamlet12.ppt

1. Click Slide 4 on the Slides tab, double-click Shakespeare, click the Insert Hyperlink button 🖲 on the toolbar, click Existing File or Web Page in the Link to bar, type www.shakespeare.org.uk/ in the Address box, click OK, then click the slide to deselect the text and see the hyperlink *See Figure 4-31*.

2. Click Slide 5-Actors in the Slides tab, drag to select the text Jennifer Laina, click the Insert Hyperlink button 🖲, click Place in This Document in the Link to bar, then click Slide 8 Jennifer in the Select a place in this document box *See Figure 4-32*.

3. Click OK to close the dialog box

4. Click Slide 1, click the Show (from current slide) button 🖵, press [Spacebar] three times, then click the Shakespeare link If you were connected to the Internet, the page will open in your browser.

5. Close the browser to return to the PowerPoint slide show, press [Spacebar], click the Jennifer Laina link, press [Spacebar], then press [ESC]

 close Hamlet12.ppt

Hyperlinks are active only when you run a presentation in Slide Show view.

Figure 4-31: Linking to an address on the Web

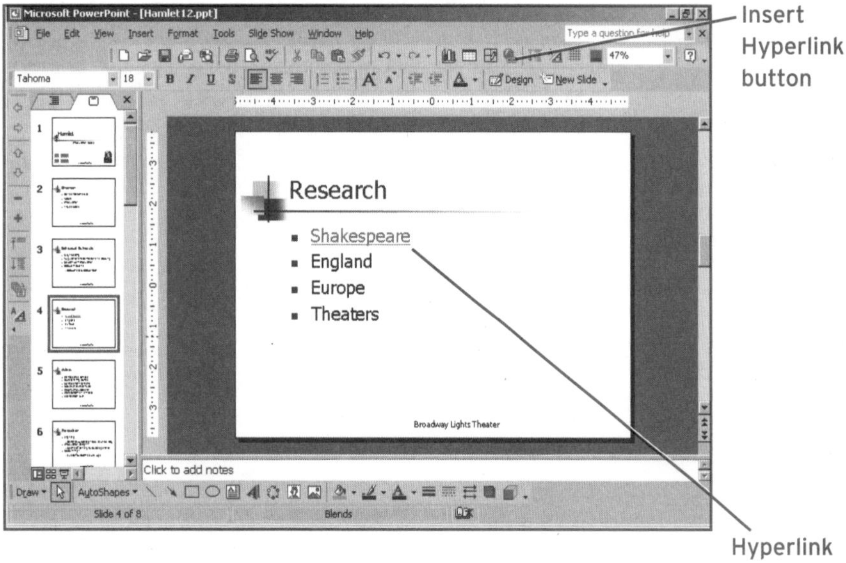

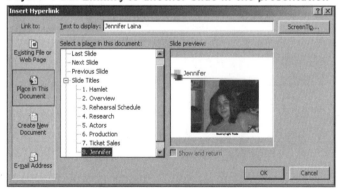

Insert Hyperlink button

Hyperlink

Figure 4-32: Linking to another slide in the presentation

extra!

Using Action Buttons

An action button is a premade button that you can use to create hyperlinks for commonly used activities such as navigating among slides and playing sounds or video. To create an action button, click Slide Show on the menu bar, point to Action Buttons, click the desired Action Button, then drag to create the action button on the slide. Specify what you want the button to do in the Action Settings dialog box that opens, then click OK. As with all hyperlinks, action buttons work only in Slide Show view.

Skill Set 4

Modifying Presentation Formats

Target Your Skills

 open Funding1.ppt

1 Use Figure 4-33 as a guide. Apply the Neutron Animation scheme to slide 1, and Grow and exit to slides 4 and 5. Set the transition for slide 1 to a slow Checkerboard Across, for slides 2-5 to Fast Newsflash. Rehearse, inserting appropriate timings for each slide. Verify that the links work.

Figure 4-33

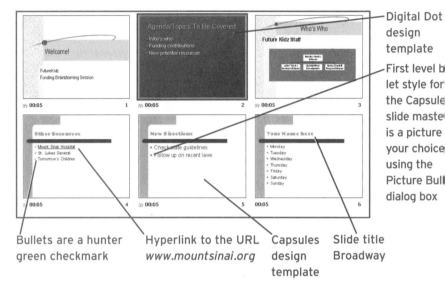

Bullets are a hunter green checkmark

Hyperlink to the URL *www.mountsinai.org*

Capsules design template

Slide title Broadway

Digital Dot design template

First level bullet style for the Capsule slide master is a picture your choice using the Picture Bullet dialog box

 open Ppretzel1.ppt

2 Use Figure 4-34 as a guide. Delete the existing default template. Apply the Compress animation scheme to all slides. Set show to have a Fade Smoothly transition automatically after 3 seconds. Then set other transition times between each slide.

Figure 4-34

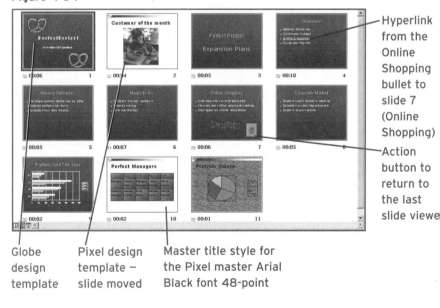

Globe design template

Pixel design template – slide moved

Master title style for the Pixel master Arial Black font 48-point

Hyperlink from the Online Shopping bullet to slide 7 (Online Shopping)

Action button to return to the last slide viewed

Skill List

1. Preview and print slides, outlines, handouts, and speaker notes

Though you will often want to give a presentation by projecting your slides on a screen, you might also want to print them. In this skill set you will learn how to preview and print your PowerPoint slides as well as various support materials in the presentation, such as the outlines, notes, and comments. You will also learn how to create handouts for your audience and speaker notes for yourself.

Skill Set 5

Preview and Print Slides, Outlines, Handouts, and Speaker Notes
Preview Slides

It's a good idea to preview your slides before you actually print them. Your presentations can have many slides, and printing can use up a lot of paper. To see how the printout will look using the current print settings, click the Print Preview button on the Standard toolbar. You can also click Preview in the Print dialog box to see how the settings will affect your printout.

When you click the Print Preview command, the Preview window opens and displays a preview of your printed slides. You can use the Previous Page and Next Page buttons to view each slide, and you can use the Zoom list arrow to view your slides at any magnification. You can specify what you want to print, and can use the Options drop-down list to frame each slide.

Activity Steps

 open Avivamkt1.ppt

You can view Slides, Handouts, Notes, and Outlines in the Preview window.

1. Click the **Print Preview button** on the toolbar
   See Figure 5-1. If your printer settings specify a black-and-white printer, the slides will appear in grayscale. If your printer settings specify a color printer, you will see the slides in color.

2. Click the **Next Page button** on the Preview toolbar

3. Click the **Previous Page button** on the toolbar, click the **Options list arrow**, then click **Frame Slides**

4. Click the **Next Page button** four times on the toolbar, click the ⊕ on the **Working on the Web! WordArt**, click the **Zoom list arrow**, then click **Fit**
   See Figure 5-2.

5. Click the **Close button** on the toolbar.

 close Avivamkt1.ppt

---

extra!

Getting to the Preview Window
There are many ways to open the Preview window. In Normal or Slide Sorter view you can click File on the menu bar, then click Print Preview. You can click the Print Preview button on the Standard toolbar, or you can click Preview in the Print dialog box.

Figure 5-1: Preview window

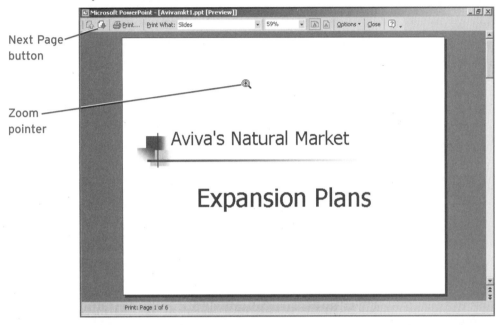

Next Page button

Zoom pointer

Figure 5-2: Preview window with framed slide

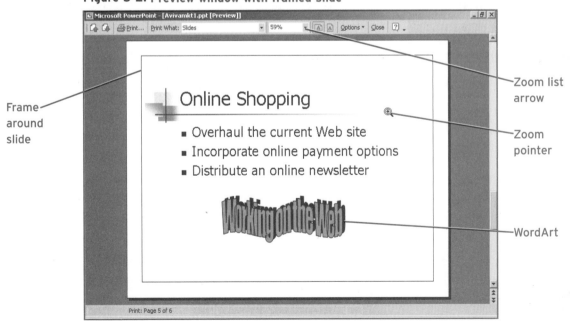

Frame around slide

Zoom list arrow

Zoom pointer

WordArt

Skill Set 5

Printing Presentations

Preview and Print Slides, Outlines, Handouts, and Speaker Notes
Print Slides

To print a presentation, you can use the Print button on the Standard Toolbar to print the slides with the default settings. If you want to change the print settings before you print, use the Print command on the File menu to open the Print dialog box. This dialog box lets you specify whether to print slides, notes, handouts, or an outline of your presentation. You can also specify which slides to print, whether to print them in landscape or portrait orientation, how many copies to print, and whether to collate the copies or not. If you have a color printer you can also stipulate whether to print in color, grayscale, or black and white.

You can select specific slides and the order in which they print by clicking the Slides option button in the Print Range area of the Print dialog box. Type the slide numbers separated by commas in the Slides box. Consecutive slides can be entered with a dash.

Activity Steps

 open Avivamkt2.ppt

1. Click **File** on the menu bar, then click **Print**
   The Print dialog box opens.

2. Click the **Slides option button** in the Print range section, then type **1-2,4-6**

3. Click the **Color/grayscale list arrow**, then click **Grayscale**

4. Verify that **1** is in the Number of copies box, then verify that **Slides** is in the Print what box
   See Figure 5-3.

5. Click **OK**

6. Click **Slide 3**, click **File** on the menu bar, click **Print**, click the **Current slide option button**, click the **Color/grayscale list arrow**, click **Color**, then click **OK**
   If you have a printer connected to your computer, slide 3 will print in grayscale.

 close Avivamkt2.ppt

Figure 5-3: The Print dialog box

Your printer will probably be different

Specifies which slides will print

Specifies the slides will print in grayscale even if you have a color printer

Number of copies

Click to frame slides

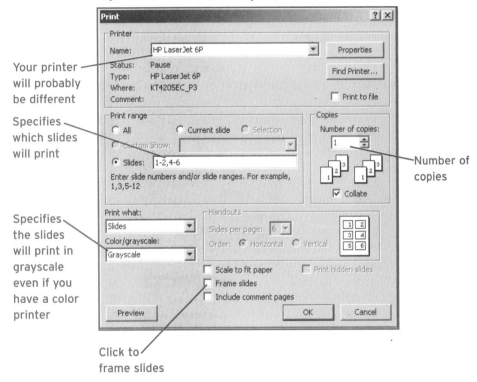

extra!

Creating a summary slide

You can create a summary slide that includes all the titles from a selection of slides as a bulleted list. When you want to present your slides, this slide can be very helpful in providing your audience with an overview of key points in your presentation. From Slide Sorter View, click to select the slides that you want included in the summary slide, then click the Summary Slide button on the toolbar. The slide is created automatically and placed at the beginning of your presentation. You can move or modify it as necessary.

Skill Set 5

Printing Presentations

Preview and Print Slides, Outlines, Handouts, and Speaker Notes
Preview and Print Outlines

Sometimes it's helpful to view and print only the text of your presentation without having to print every slide. The Outline tab displays all the text in your presentation, except for any text entered in text boxes or AutoShapes. Printing the outline is a good way to focus on the words of your presentation; it can save paper, too. You can print the outline at any time and control various factors that determine how it looks as a printed document.

To set up slide sizes for printing on special paper, click File on the menu bar, click Page Setup, then specify the paper size in the Slides sized for box, or enter sizing for a custom width and height.

Activity Steps

 open Avivamkt3.ppt

1. Click **File** on the menu bar, then click **Print**

2. Click the **Print what list arrow**, then click **Outline View**

3. Click **Preview**
   See Figure 5-4.

4. Click the **Landscape button** on the toolbar
   See Figure 5-5.

5. Click the **Print button** 🖨, then click **OK** in the Print dialog box

 close Avivamkt3.ppt

Figure 5-4: Outline in Preview window—portrait orientation

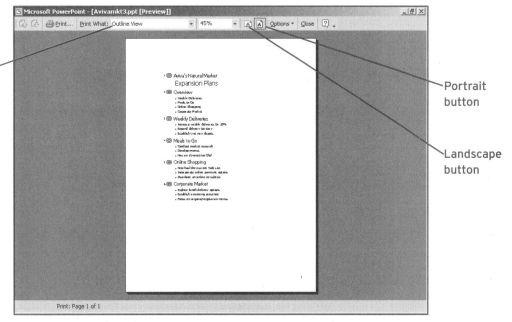

Outline View displayed in Print what box

Portrait button

Landscape button

Figure 5-5: Outline in Preview window—landscape orientation

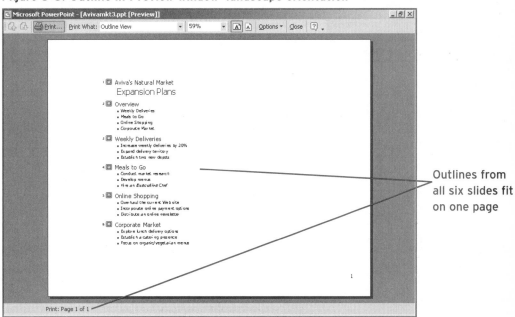

Outlines from all six slides fit on one page

Skill Set 5
Printing Presentations

Preview and Print Slides, Outlines, Handouts, and Speaker Notes
Preview and Print Handouts

Handouts are printed versions of your presentation that contain one or more slides on each page. You can use handouts to help your audience follow your presentation. You have many options for organizing the slides on the handout pages. You can print up to nine slides per page. If your presentation contains **hidden slides**, slides that you chose not to show or print for a particular audience, you can select whether or not to include them in the handouts. You can also select which slides print and the order in which they print.

The Handout Master shows how the slides will be positioned and lets you change the header and footer. To view the Handout Master, click View on the menu bar, click Master, then click Handout Master.

Activity Steps

 open Avivamkt4.ppt

1. Click **File** on the menu bar, then click **Print**

2. Click the **Print what list arrow**, then click **Handouts**

3. Click the **Slides per page list arrow** in the Handouts area, then click **3**

4. Click **Preview**
   See Figure 5-6.

5. Click the **Print What list arrow**, then click **Handouts (6 slides per page)**
   See Figure 5-7.

6. Click the **Options list arrow**, click **Frame slides** to remove the frames, review the difference, click **Options list arrow**, then click **Frame slides** to turn it on

7. Click the **Print button** , then click **OK** in the Print dialog box

 close Avivamkt4.ppt

Figure 5-6: Handouts with three slides per page in Preview window

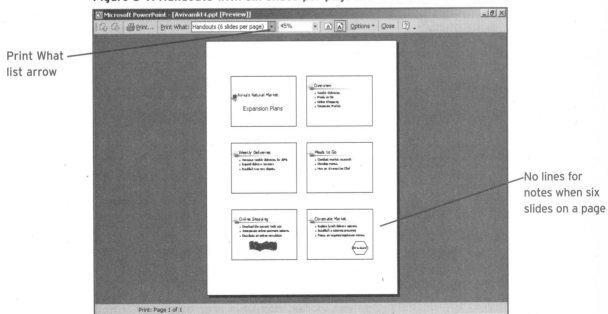

Portrait button

Lines for notes

Three slides on each page

Handout will be two pages

Each slide is framed

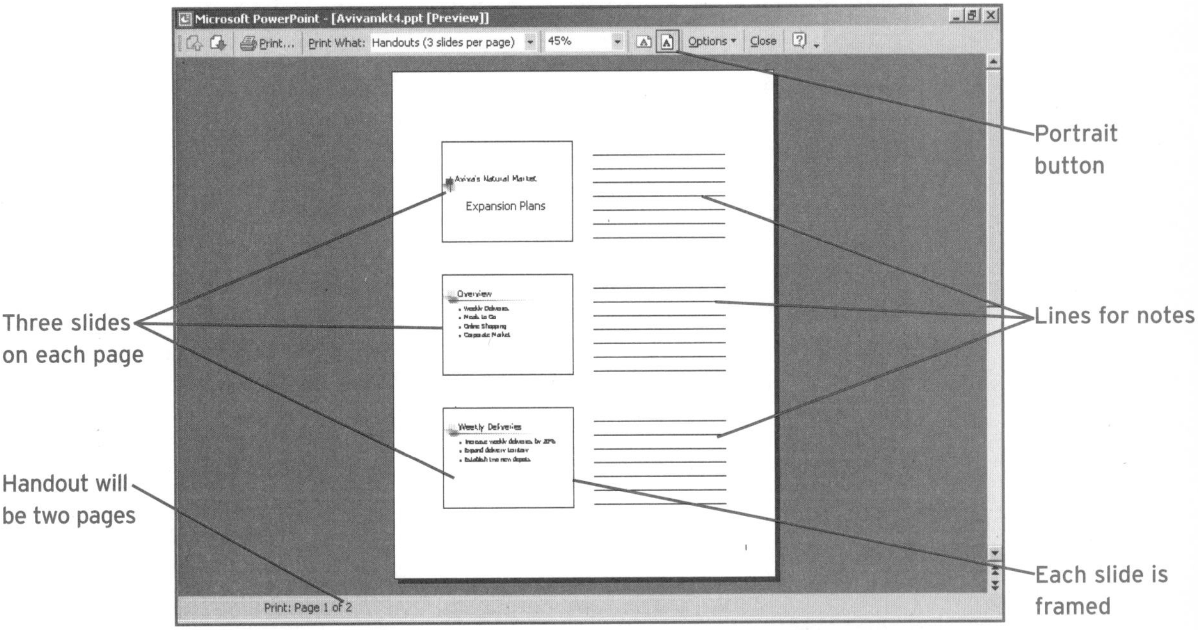

Figure 5-7: Handouts with six slides per page in Preview window

Print What list arrow

No lines for notes when six slides on a page

Skill Set 5

Printing Presentations

Preview and Print Slides, Outlines, Handouts, and Speaker Notes
Preview and Print Speaker Notes

When you're in front of an audience giving a presentation, it's helpful to have notes on hand to remind you what to say about each slide. In PowerPoint, notes pages contain a picture of the slide with your notes underneath. You enter your notes in the Notes pane in Normal view. You can view these on the computer as you deliver the presentation if you use multiple monitors, or print them out to help you or others prepare for the presentation. You can apply text formatting to notes to make them easier to read, and you can even add pictures or objects. To make global changes to the notes page layout or to add a logo or text that you want to appear on all the notes, add it to the notes master. You can specify the default formatting of your notes, such as font or bullet styles, on the master.

Use the Print dialog box to print on various sized paper, overheads, or banners. You can print to a file rather than to a printer, and you can also find a printer on the Web.

Activity Steps

 open Avivamkt5.ppt

1. Click **View** on the menu bar, point to **Master**, then click **Notes Master**

2. Click **File** on the menu bar, then click **Print**

3. Click the **Print what list arrow**, then click **Notes Pages**

4. If you have a color printer, click the **Name list arrow** in the Printer section, select the color printer, click the **Color/grayscale list arrow**, then click **Color**
   See Figure 5-8.

5. Click **Preview**, then click the **Next Page button** four times to display slide 5
   See Figure 5-9.

6. Click the **Print button** , then click **OK** in the Print dialog box

 close Avivamkt5.ppt

Figure 5-8: Print dialog box for printing notes pages on a color printer

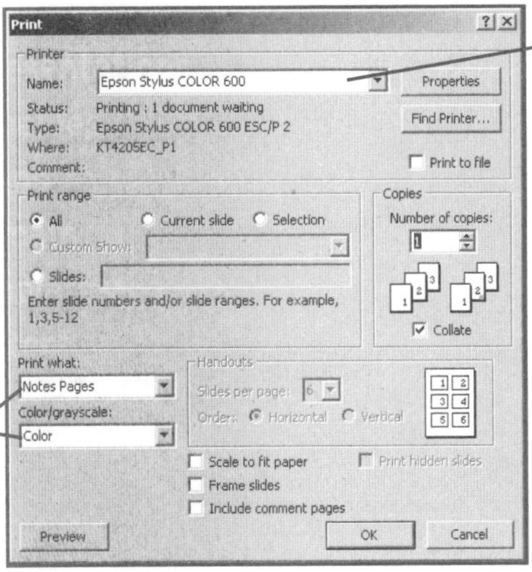

Color printer selected; your printer will probably be different

Notes Pages will print in color

Figure 5-9: Notes page in Preview window

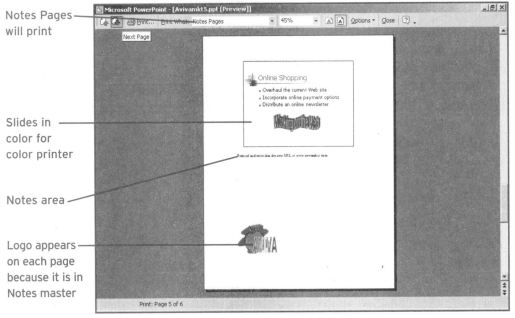

Notes Pages will print

Slides in color for color printer

Notes area

Logo appears on each page because it is in Notes master

Skill Set 5

Printing Presentations

Preview and Print Slides, Outlines, Handouts, and Speaker Notes
Print Comments Pages

If you work with several people to create a presentation, you might want to insert comments to communicate your ideas or concerns about particular slides to the other people on the team. They, in turn, can add their own comments for you to review. Comments appear as yellow popup boxes on the slide with the reviewer's initials identifying each comment. If you point to the small box with the initials, a larger box will open to display the comment. You can print the comments as part of the slides, handouts, or notes.

Activity Steps

 open Avivamkt6.ppt

Click the Insert Comment button on the Reviewing toolbar, then type any notes to add a comment to any slide.

1. Click **Slide 3**, click **View** on the menu bar, point to **Toolbars**, then verify that there is a checkmark next to **Reviewing** (if there is no checkmark, click Reviewing to open the Reviewing toolbar)

2. Click outside the menu, then place the pointer over the **comment** in slide 3 to expand the comment
See Figure 5-10.

3. Click **File** on the menu bar, then click **Print**

4. Click the **Print what list arrow**, click **Slides**, then verify that the **All option button** in the Print range area is selected

5. Click the **Include comment pages check box**, click **Preview**, click the **Next Page button** to display the comments page for slide 1, then click **Options** on the toolbar
The Options list shows that Include Comments Pages is selected, as shown in Figure 5-11.

6. Click the **Print button**, then click **OK** in the Print dialog box

 close Avivamkt6.ppt

Figure 5-10: Viewing a comment

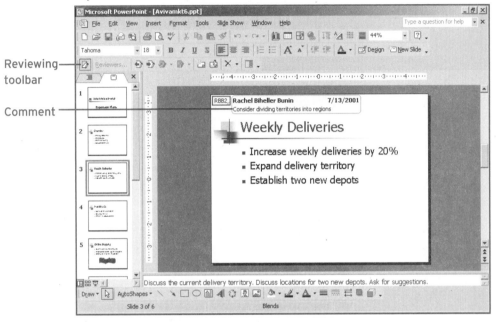

Figure 5-11: Comment page in Preview window

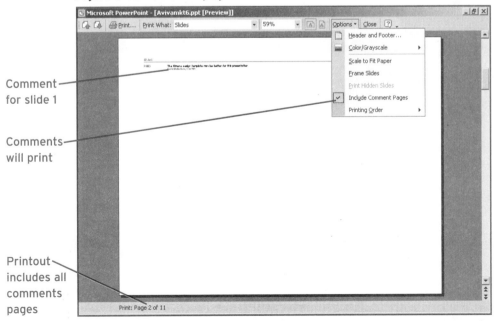

Skill Set 5

Printing Presentations

Target Your Skills

 open Jjewels1.ppt

1 Use Figure 5-12 as a guide. Preview and print handouts containing all the slides. First print the handouts with 6 slides per page, then print the handouts with three slides per page. Finally, preview and print one copy of Slides 1, 3, and 5.

Figure 5-12

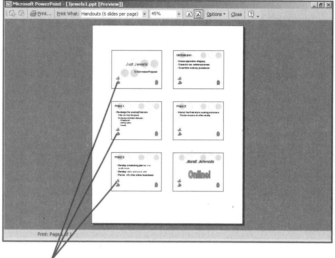

Slides 1, 3, and 5

 open Springrecipes1.ppt

2 Use Figure 5-13 as a guide to preview and print the Notes pages. Be sure to include Comments Pages and frame the slides. There are several comments throughout the presentation and each slide has a note. After you print the Notes pages, preview and print the outline for this presentation. Include all the slides in each of the printouts.

Figure 5-13

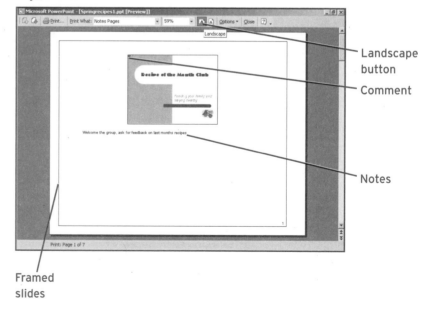

Landscape button

Comment

Notes

Framed slides

126   Certification Circle

Skill List

1. Import Excel charts to slides
2. Add sound and video to slides
3. Insert Word tables on slides
4. Export a presentation as an outline

When you create a presentation, you often want to display data on your slides for discussion and analysis. For instance, you might want to insert a chart or table to show sales trends, budgets, marketing results, or projections. PowerPoint is a presentation tool, not an analysis tool, so it's best to create these objects in other programs and then insert them into your presentation. In this skill set, you will learn how to use PowerPoint to incorporate data from other sources. You will learn to insert Word tables, Excel charts, and video and sound files into your slides. You'll also learn how to save a presentation as an RTF file so that it can be opened in other programs, making it easier to collaborate with colleagues.

Skill Set 6

Working with Data from Other Sources

Import Excel Charts to Slides

Embed Excel Charts on Slides

A picture is worth a thousand words, especially when presenting numeric data. You can add an Excel chart to your presentation by embedding it as an object. **Embedding** means inserting an object created in another program, called a **source program**, into your presentation. Once you embed an object into a presentation, the object becomes part of the presentation file and no longer has a connection to the **source file**, where the object was originally created. The embedded object does stay connected to the source program, however. Clicking the embedded object activates the source program so you can make changes to the object using the source program's tools. Changes to the object in the presentation file (known as the **destination file**, because it contains the embedded object) are not reflected in the source file. Changes made to the object in the source file are not updated in the destination file. You embed an Excel chart using the Insert Object dialog box.

Activity Steps

 open Famfarm1.ppt

1. Click **Slide 7**, click **Insert** on the menu bar, then click **Object** to open the Insert Object dialog box
   See Figure 6-1.

2. Click the **Create from file option button** in the Insert Object dialog box, click **Browse**, locate the folder containing your Project Files, click **Famfarm1.xls**, then click **OK**
   The path to the source file Famfarm1.xls appears in the Insert Object dialog box.

3. Click **OK**
   A worksheet and chart appear in the slide as an embedded object.

4. Use the ⬚ pointer to drag the chart to the right, as shown in Figure 6-2

5. Double click the **chart** to open the embedded chart and workbook in Excel, click the **Zoom list arrow** (you may have to click the Toolbar Options button ⬚ to display the Zoom button), then click **100%**

6. Click **WashDC** in cell E2 of the worksheet, type **MetroDC**, press **[Enter]**, type **8800** in cell E3, then click the slide
   The changes appear in the chart legend and in the data. Because this is an embedded chart, the changes will not appear in the source file.

 close Famfarm1.ppt

To create an Excel chart in PowerPoint, click Insert on the menu bar, click Object, verify that the Create new option button is selected, select Microsoft Excel Chart, then click OK.

Figure 6-1: Insert Object dialog box

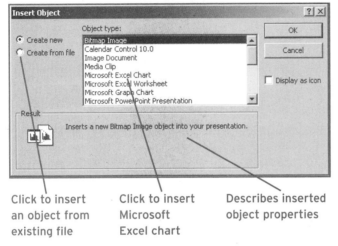

Click to insert
an object from
existing file

Click to insert
Microsoft
Excel chart

Describes inserted
object properties

Figure 6-2: Slide with embedded Excel chart

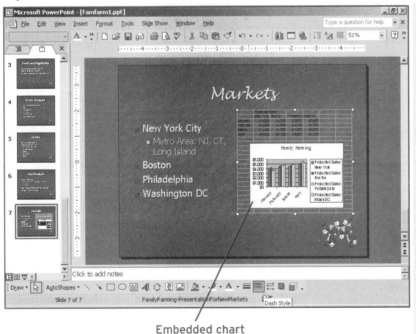

Embedded chart

extra!

**Embedding part
of a file**

Using the Insert Object
command embeds an
entire Excel workbook
into your presentation,
which could contain
multiple worksheets
and charts. If you want
to insert only a part of
an Excel workbook (for
instance only a chart),
open the workbook in
Excel, right-click the
chart, then click Copy.
Next, open your pres-
entation in PowerPoint,
select the slide where
you want to insert the
object, click Edit on the
menu bar, click Paste
Special, select the Paste
option button, click
Microsoft Excel Chart
Object, then click OK.

Skill Set 6

Working with Data from Other Sources

Import Excel Charts to Slides
Link Excel Charts to Slides

If you want the Excel chart you have inserted into your presentation to be updated every time a change is made to the source file, you can link it to the source file. **Linking** an object means that you set up a connection between the inserted object and the source file; any changes made to the object in the source file are reflected in the object in the destination file. You link objects when you want updates in the source file to be reflected in the presentation or updates in the linked object to be reflected in the source file. To link a chart in Excel to a PowerPoint presentation, you first open the Excel worksheet and copy the chart you want to insert. Then you open the presentation and use the Paste Link command to insert the chart as a linked object. The linked object appears in the presentation and is a shortcut to the source file in the source program. If you work with active data that changes regularly, inserting linked objects in your slides will ensure that your presentation contains the most up-to-date numbers.

Step 5
To view all the linked objects in a presentation, click Edit on the menu bar, then click Links to open the Links dialog box. Use this dialog box to set the update to Automatic or Manual, to change a source, to update manual links, or to break a connection to a linked object.

Activity Steps

 open Famfarm2.ppt

1. Start **Microsoft Excel**, click **File** on the menu bar, click **Open**, navigate to the folder containing your Project Files, click **Famfarm2.xls**, then click **Open**
   An Excel worksheet opens with data in cells A1:B6 and a pie chart below the data.

2. Click the **border of the chart** to select the chart and open the Chart toolbar, click **Edit** on the menu bar, then click **Copy**

3. Click the **Microsoft PowerPoint button** on the taskbar, click **Slide 5**, click **Edit** on the menu bar, click **Paste Special**, verify that **Microsoft Excel Chart Object** is selected in the As: box, then click the **Paste link** option button
   See Figure 6-3.

4. Click **OK** (if the chart covers the text box, move it to the right)

5. Right-click the **chart**, point to **Linked Worksheet Object**, click **Open** on the shortcut menu to open the source file, click **300** in cell B2, type **700**, then press **[Enter]**

6. Click the **PowerPoint button** on the taskbar, click the **Zoom list arrow** on the toolbar, then click **100%**
   The White and brown rice pie segment has changed to 700 corresponding to the changes you made in the source file. *See Figure 6-4.*

 close Famfarm2.ppt

Figure 6-3: Paste Special dialog box

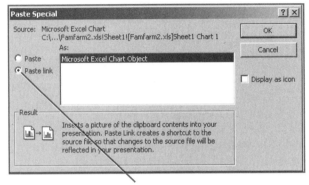

Click to paste Excel
chart as a linked object

Figure 6-4: Slide with linked Excel chart

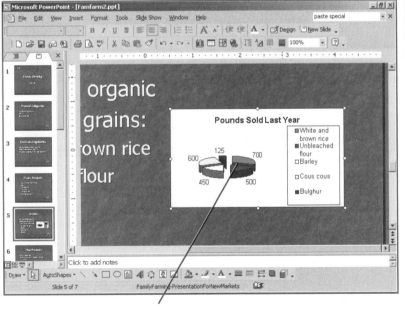

Linked chart shows
updated data

extra!

Linking Objects from within PowerPoint

You can also insert linked objects into a presentation without having to open the source file. To link a worksheet from within PowerPoint, click Insert on the menu bar, then click Object to open the Insert Object dialog box. Click the Create from file option button in the Insert Object dialog box, click Browse, locate the source .xls file, click the Link check box, then click OK. An image of the worksheet with the chart appears in the slide. It's important to note that inserting an object this way inserts the entire file into your presentation. If you want to link only a portion of a file, you need to copy the object from within the source program, then use the Paste Special command to paste it into the presentation.

Skill Set 6

Working with Data from Other Sources

Add Sound and Video to Slides
Add Sound Effects to Slides

There's nothing like sound to give life to your presentation. A **sound file** can be music, a speech, or a sound effect such as a train whistle, rocket noise, or bells. Sound can create a mood; you can insert a sound to make a point, amuse the audience, or demonstrate an effect. The sound file can play automatically when the slide appears or when you click the slide. PowerPoint has many ways to insert sound effects into a presentation. Most sound files have a .wav or an .mp3 file extension. You can create your own sounds if your computer is set up to record sound, or you can insert the many sound files that come with Office in the Clip Organizer.

Step 2
To select a sound file from the Clip Organizer, click Insert point to Movies and Sounds, then click Sound from Clip Organizer to open the Insert Clip Art task pane. You can also insert a sound file by applying a slide layout that includes a Media Clip, then clicking the Media Clip icon and choosing a sound file from the Media Clip dialog box.

Activity Steps

 open Famfarm3.ppt

1. Click **Slide 3**, click **Insert** on the menu bar, point to **Movies and Sounds**, then click **Sound from File**

2. Locate the folder where your Project Files are stored, click **cheers.wav** in the Insert Sound dialog box, click **OK**, click **Yes** to play the sound automatically in the slide show, then drag the **sound icon** to the middle of the line below the last bullet item
See Figure 6-5. If you get a message to install the feature for the instructions in step 2, follow the instructions to install it.

3. Click **Slide 6**, click **Slide Show** on the menu bar, click **Slide Transition** to open the Slide Transition task pane, click the **Sound list arrow** in the Modify transition section, click **Drum Roll**, click the **Automatically after** check box, then set the timer to **00:03**
See Figure 6-6.

4. Click **Slide 1**, click the **Slide Show (from current slide) button**, then press **[Enter]** as many times as needed to advance through the slide show and return to Normal view
If a sound card and speakers are attached to your computer, you will hear two sounds as you advance through the slides.

close Famfarm3.ppt

Figure 6-5: Sound clip inserted in slide

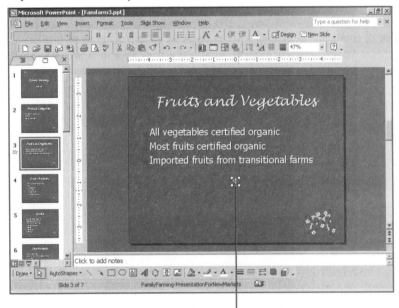

Icon for sound file

Figure 6-6: Sound specifications in Slide Transition task pane

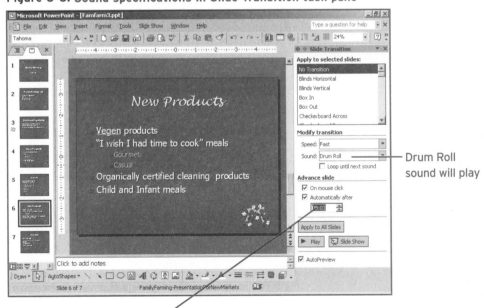

Drum Roll sound will play

Timer set for 3 seconds

Skill Set 6

Working with Data from Other Sources

Add Sound and Video to Slides
Add Video Effects to Slides

Static images go only so far when you need to illustrate certain concepts. **Video files** show motion and could be used to make your points stronger in a variety of ways. For instance, you might insert a video clip of your company president talking about a trend, one of your customers reacting to a product, or an animation that shows a process. You can insert a ready-made media clip from the Clip Organizer or you can record digital video using you own camera and then insert it into a presentation. Video formats include AVI, QuickTime, and MPEG. You can insert any file with an .avi, .mov, .qt, .mpg, or .mpeg file extension as a video in your presentation. You can also insert **animated gif files**, which contain multiple static images that stream to create an animated effect.

Activity Steps

 open Famfarm4.ppt

1. Click **Slide 2**, click **Insert** on the menu bar, point to **Movies and Sounds**, then click **Movie from File**
   The Insert Movie dialog box opens showing all the movie file types in the files of type box.

2. Navigate to the folder containing your Project Files, click the file **globe.avi**, click **OK**, then click **No** to specify that the movie not play automatically

3. Drag the **bottom left corner handle** of the globe.avi image down and to the left to increase the size of the clip to approximately 3" square, then drag the **globe image** to the position shown in Figure 6-7

4. Right-click the **globe image**, click **Action Settings**, click the **Mouse Over tab**, click the **Object action option button**, then click **OK**

5. Click the **Slide show (from current slide) button** , then place the pointer on the **globe** image to set it in motion
   See Figure 6-8.

 close Famfarm4.ppt

Step 4
Open the Custom Animation task pane to change the animation effects for the video, including the trigger and speed.

Figure 6-7: Video inserted on slide

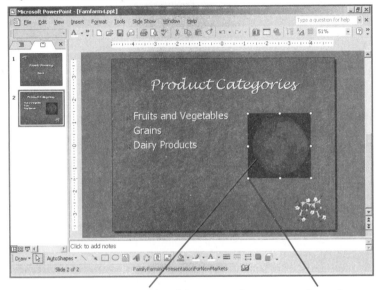

Globe.avi video in slide   Drag corner to resize

Figure 6-8: Video in motion

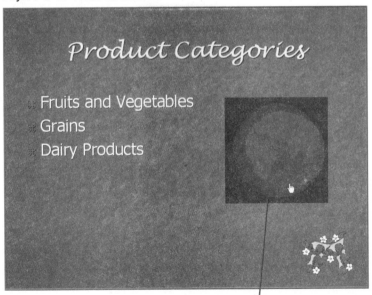

Video in motion with mouse positioned over it

extra!

Using the Media Clip Slide Layout

You can also insert a video on a slide by selecting a layout that includes the Media Clip icon. You'll find one of these in the Other Layouts section of the Slide Layout task pane. Double-click the Media Clip icon on the slide layout to open the Media Clip dialog box. To search for a particular clip, type a keyword in the Search box, then click Search. Click a clip to insert it into your presentation. To import a media clip, click the Import button, then click the file you want to import.

Skill Set 6

Working with Data from Other Sources

Insert Word Tables on Slides
Embed Word Tables on Slides

Even though PowerPoint has the ability to create native tables, it's sometimes easier to insert an existing Word table in your presentation. If you are not concerned about maintaining a connection between the table in the presentation and the source file (the Word file where it was created), you can embed the table. When you embed a table, changes to the table in the presentation are not reflected in the source file and vice versa. When you double-click the table in PowerPoint, you activate Word and can make changes to the table using Word's tools. To embed a Word table in a presentation, you use the Insert Object dialog box to specify the name and location of the Word file you want to embed.

Activity Steps

 open Famfarm5.ppt

1. Click **Slide 3**, click **Insert** on the menu bar, then click **Object** to open the Insert Object dialog box

2. Click the **Create from file option button** in the Insert Object dialog box, click **Browse**, navigate to the folder containing your Project Files, click **Famfarm5.doc**, then click **OK**
   The Insert Object dialog box shows the path to the file Famfarm5.doc in the File box. This file contains the Word table you want to insert.

3. Click **OK**, then resize the table so it is slightly larger and centered on the slide

4. Double-click the **embedded table** on the slide to activate Word
   See Figure 6-9.

5. Click the **Zoom list arrow** on the toolbar, click **100%**, select **WashDC**, type **Metro DC**, press **[Tab]** five times to select **$3,800**, type **$8,800**, click the slide, click the **Zoom list arrow** on the toolbar, click **50%**
   See Figure 6-10. The change is made only to the table on the slide. No change is made to the source file.

 close Famfarm5.ppt

Step 3
When you resize the table, be careful to drag a corner handle to retain the proportions for the height and width.

Figure 6-9: Embedded table in slide with Word activated

Your toolbars may be docked differently

Word table embedded in slide with Word activated

Zoom list arrow

Word toolbars are integrated in PowerPoint so you can edit the embedded object

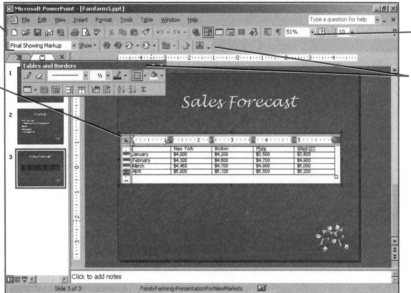

Figure 6-10: Edited table in slide

Edited Word table

Changes to text

Skill Set 6

Working with Data from Other Sources

Insert Word Tables on Slides
Link Word Tables on Slides

Just as you can link an Excel chart to a slide in a presentation, you can also insert a Word table as a linked object on a slide. As outlined above, a **linked object** is one that maintains a connection with the source file where it was created, so that when changes are made in the source file, those changes are reflected in the linked object. You link Word tables when you want updates in the source file to be reflected in the presentation or updates in the linked object to be reflected back in the source file. To add a linked table to a PowerPoint slide, click Insert on the menu bar, then click Object to open the Insert Object dialog box. Specify the location of the document containing the table, click the Link check box, then click OK to insert the linked table. The table appears in the presentation. Double-clicking the table in the presentation opens the source file in Word, where you can make changes to it.

Activity Steps

 open Famfarm6.ppt

1. Click **Slide 3**, click **Insert** on the menu bar, then click **Object** to open the Insert Object dialog box

2. Click the **Create from file option button** in the Insert Object dialog box, click **Browse**, navigate to the folder containing your Project Files, click **Famfarm6.doc**, then click **OK** in the Browse dialog box
   The Insert Object dialog box shows the path to the file Farmfarm6.doc in the File box. This file contains the Word table that you want to link.

3. Click the **Link check box**

4. Click **OK**, then resize the object so it is slightly larger and centered on the slide

5. Right-click the **table object**, point to **Linked Document Object**, then click **Edit**
   The source file Famfarm6.doc opens in Microsoft Word. *See Figure 6-11.*

6. Double-click **1000**, type **700**, double-click **6000**, then type **500**

7. Click the **PowerPoint button** on the taskbar, right click the **table**, then click **Update Link**
   The table is updated in the slide. *See Figure 6-12.*

 close Famfarm6.ppt

If the source document for a linked table has been moved, renamed, or deleted, click Edit on the menu bar, click Links, click Change Source, then click the new location of the source file.

Figure 6-11: Document opens in Microsoft Word

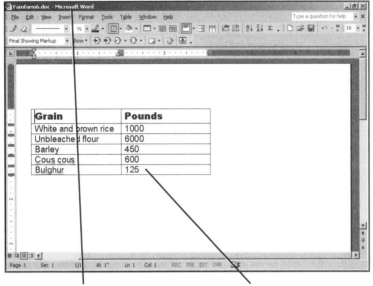

Source file open in Microsoft Word   Table

Figure 6-12: Linked table is updated

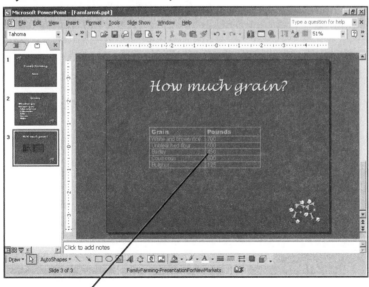

Linked data is updated in slide

extra!

Using Paste Special
To use Paste Special
to link a Word table,
select the table in
Word, click Edit on
the Word toolbar,
click Copy, click the
slide in PowerPoint,
click Edit on the
menu bar, then click
Paste Special. Click
the Paste Link option
button in the Paste
Special dialog box,
click Microsoft Word
Document Object,
then click OK. Using
Paste Special inserts
just the copied object;
using the Insert
Object inserts the
entire document.

Skill Set 6

Working with Data from Other Sources

Export a Presentation as an Outline
Saving Slide Presentations as RTF Outlines

If you work with colleagues who do not have access to Microsoft Office but would like to view the text from your presentation using another application, you can save the text as an RTF file. **Rich Text Format (RTF) files** can easily be imported or transferred between other application formats. However, when you save a presentation as RTF, you lose any graphics or media files that were part of the original file. The text does retain formatting such as font type and font style.

Activity Steps

 open Famfarm7.ppt

1. Click **File** on the menu bar, then click **Save As**

2. Click the **Save as type list arrow**, then click **Outline/RTF (*.rtf)**
   See Figure 6-13.

3. Click **Save**

4. Click the **Start button** on the task bar, point to **Programs**, point to **Accessories**, click **Windows Explorer**, then navigate to the folder where your Project Files are stored

5. Double-click **Famfarm7.rtf**
   The file opens in Word showing all the text with formatting from the original presentation.

6. Click **View** on the Word menu bar to be sure you are in Normal view
   See Figure 6-14.

7. Scroll to view both pages of the document file

 close Famfarm7.ppt

Step 5
If the Famfarm7.rtf file does not have a Word icon, rtf files are not associated with Word on your computer. Right-click Famfarm7.rtf in the Explorer window, click Open With, then click Microsoft Word in the Open With dialog box.

Figure 6-13: Save as RTF file

Save as
Outline/RTF
file

Figure 6-14: Famfarm7.rtf open in Word

Text
formatting
from
presentation

Bullet
formatting
from
presentation

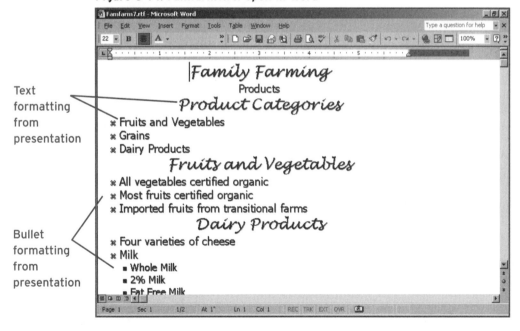

Skill Set 6

Working with Data from Other Sources

Target Your Skills

 open Pan1.ppt

1 Use Figure 6-15 as a guide to enhance the presentation. Edit the table in Microsoft Word so that the June matinee show begins at 2:30. Update the link in the presentation. Go back to the Pan1.doc file in Word, change the June matinee time back to 2pm, then use the Update Link command to update the table on the slide. Run the slide show.

Figure 6-15

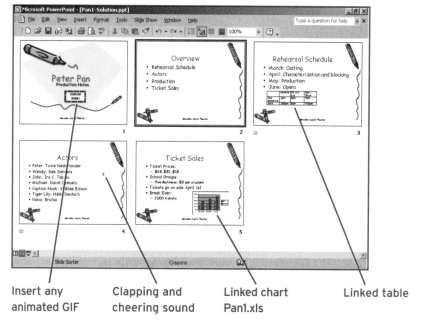

Insert any animated GIF — Clapping and cheering sound — Linked chart Pan1.xls — Linked table

 open Retreat1.ppt

2 Use Figure 6-16 as a guide to enhance the presentation. Save the presentation as an RTF outline. Run the slide show, making sure to place the pointer on the video image on slide 4 to view the animation. View the RTF file in Word.

Figure 6-16

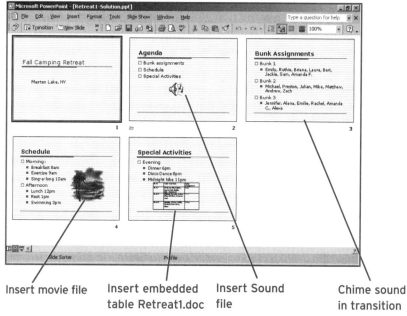

Insert movie file — Insert embedded table Retreat1.doc — Insert Sound file — Chime sound in transition

Skill List

1. Set up slide shows
2. Deliver presentations
3. Manage files and folders for presentations
4. Work with embedded fonts
5. Publish presentations to the Web
6. Use Pack and Go

Once you have completed a presentation, you are ready to set it up for delivery. Showing your finished slides to an audience is the goal of creating a presentation. You can run your slide show on your computer using one or two monitors. With special equipment, you can use your computer like a projector to show your presentation in a large room. In this skill set, you'll learn to use PowerPoint to accommodate almost any presentation situation. You'll learn how to set up a slide show so that it runs according to your specifications, embed fonts to make sure that all fonts appear on the slides, and create a custom slide show that displays only selected slides for a specific audience. You'll learn how to add discussion notes to slides in Slide Show view and how to use a drawing tool to highlight important points. You'll also learn how to save your presentation as an HTML file so that it can be viewed over the Web, and how to package your presentation so it can be delivered on a kiosk or a computer that may or may not have PowerPoint installed.

Skill Set 7

Managing and Delivering Presentations

Set Up Slide Shows
Set Up Presentations for Delivery

The hard work is done. All text and graphics are in place. Now it's time to get the presentation ready to deliver. You set the specifications for how you want to deliver the presentation in the Set Up Show dialog box. If you have the appropriate hardware and the option to use two or more monitors, you can set up the show for multiple monitors.

Step 4
Click the scroll box to display a ScreenTip that shows the current slide title and number out of the total number of slides in the presentation.

Activity Steps

 open Annie1.ppt

1. Click **Slide Show** on the menu bar, then click **Set Up Show** to open the Set Up Show dialog box

2. Click the **Browsed by an individual (window) option button**, verify that the **Show scrollbar check box** has a check mark, then click the **Manually option button** in the Advance slides section
   See Figure 7-1.

3. Click **OK**

4. Verify that Slide 1 is selected, click the **Slide Show from current slide button** 🖳, then click the **down scroll arrow** on the vertical scroll bar as many times as necessary to watch the entire slide show and return to Normal view

5. Click **Slide Show** on the menu bar, click **Set Up Show** to open the Set Up Show dialog box, click the **Presented by a speaker (full screen) option button**, click the **Loop continuously until 'Esc' check box**, then click **Using timings, if present option button**

6. Click the **Use hardware graphics acceleration check box** to take advantage of any graphics card that may be in your computer, then click **OK**

7. Click the **Slide Show (from current slide) button** 🖳, press **[Pg Dn]** as many times as necessary until you loop back to Slide 1, then press **[Esc]** to end the show

 close Annie1.ppt

Figure 7-1: Set Up Show dialog box

Determines that the show will appear in a window with scroll bars

Specifies that slides will advance manually

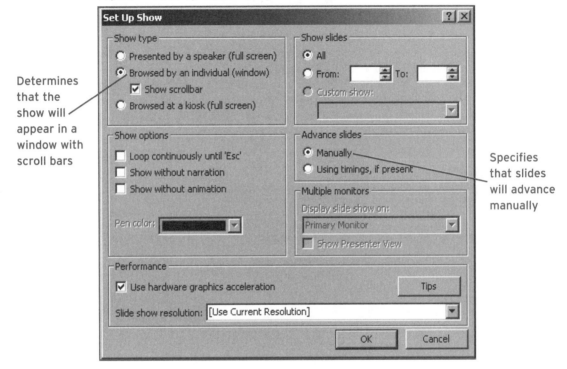

extra!

Hiding slides

For a particular audience, you might not want to show all the slides in a slide show. Rather than creating a new slide show that contains only selected slides, you can simply designate a slide (or several slides) in an existing presentation as hidden. **Hidden slides** are slides that do not display in Slide Show view. To hide selected slides, right-click any slide in Slide Sorter view or on the Slides tab in Normal view, then click Hide Slide. You can also select the slides you want to hide in Slide Sorter or Normal view, click Slide Show on the menu bar, then click Hide Slide. To hide slides using the toolbar, select the slides you want to hide, then click the Hide Slide button on the Slide Sorter toolbar. Hidden slides are marked with special icons in the Slides tab and in Slide Sorter view. The Hide Slide command is a toggle; click or select the command once to hide a slide, click it again to "unhide" a slide.

Skill Set 7

Managing and Delivering Presentations

Deliver Presentations
Prepare Slide Shows for Delivery

Before you run a slide show, you should make sure that the slide show specifications are set the way you want them. Refer to Table 7-1 for a list of ways to begin a slide show. The Show popup menu provides navigation commands and other tools to help you as the slide show is running. You use the View tab of the Options dialog box to specify whether to open the Show popup menu by right-clicking and whether to show the popup menu button on the lower left corner of the slides during the show. You can also specify whether to end the show with a black slide.

If you plan to make the slide show available on the Web or from a kiosk, you will probably want it to be self-running. To specify that the slide show will run automatically and continuously, check the Loop Continuously until 'Esc' check box in the Set Up Show dialog box.

Activity Steps

 open Annie2.ppt

1. Click **Tools** on the menu bar, click **Options** to open the Options dialog box, then click the **View tab**
   See Figure 7-2.

2. Click the **Show popup menu button** to remove the check box, then click **OK**

3. Click **Slide 1**, if not already selected, press **[F5]**, then right-click as soon as you see the Characters slide appear to stop the show and display the popup menu
   Each slide is set to advance automatically through transitions, although the popup menu button does not appear. The popup menu appears when you right-click during the show.

4. **Click anywhere on the slide to continue the show**
   The slide show will run until a black screen appears, indicating the end of the show.

5. Press **[Esc]**

 close Annie2.ppt

Figure 7-2: Options dialog box

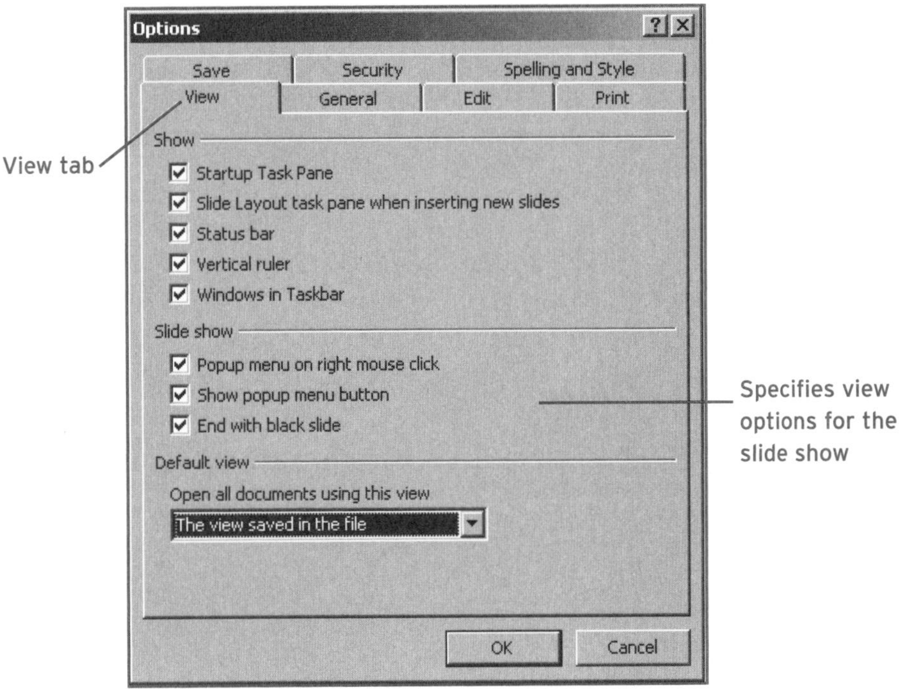

View tab

Specifies view
options for the
slide show

TABLE 7-1: Starting a slide show

From the...	To start the show....
My Computer	Right-click PPT file icon, then click Show
Windows Desktop	Right-click PPT file icon, then click Show
Windows Explorer	Right-click PPT file icon, then click Show
Power Point Normal View	• Click the Slide Show (from current slide) button • Click Slide Show on the menu bar, then click View Show • Press [F5]
Slide Transition task pane	Click the Slide Show button
Power Point Slide Sorter View	• Click the Rehearse Timings button (this is only to set the timings but will run the show) • Click Slide Show on the menu bar, then click View Show • Press [F5] • Click the Slide Show (from current slide) button
PowerPoint Show (pps file)	Double-click the pps filename

Skill Set 7

Managing and Delivering Presentations

Deliver Presentations
Run Slide Shows

There are many ways to run a slide show. If you are in Normal or Slide Sorter view, you can click the Slide Show (from current slide) button, or click View on the menu bar, then click Slide Show. You can also press [F5] from any view to start a slide show. Once you start the slide show, you can use the commands on the Show Popup menu to help you during the presentation. If you are giving a presentation during a meeting, you can use the Meeting Minder feature to keep track of meeting minutes or to record action items. You can also open Speaker Notes for individual slides to remind you about important points to make. Use the Slide Navigator to jump to a particular slide in your presentation. The Show Popup menu also lets you change Pointer Options, allowing you to end the show at any moment.

Activity Steps

 open Annie3.ppt

1. Click **Tools** on the menu bar, click **Options**, verify that the **Show popup menu button check box** has a check mark, click **OK**, verify that **Slide 1** is selected, click the **Slide Show (from current slide) button** 🖳, then press **[PgDn]** four times to display the **Characters slide**

You can set the color for the pen feature in the Set Up Show dialog box. Select a dark pen color for slides with light color backgrounds; select a light pen color for slides with dark backgrounds.

2. Place the pointer in the lower-left corner of the slide, click the **Show popup menu button** that appears, then click **Speaker Notes**
The Speaker Notes dialog box appears. *See Figure 7-3.*

3. Click **Close** on the Speaker Notes window, click the **Show popup menu button**, click **Meeting Minder**, then type **Call EastSide Casting**
See Figure 7-4.

4. Click **OK**, press **[PgDn]** to view the Production slide, click the **Show popup menu button**, point to **Pointer Options**, click **Pen**, then drag the mouse pointer to draw a circle around **Choreography**
Because the pen color was changed in the Setup show dialog box, the pointer draws like a purple pen or crayon as you move it on the screen until you end the show or press [Esc].

5. Press **[PgDn]**, draw two horizontal lines under **2,000**, type the letter **E** to erase the lines on the slide, then press **[PgUp]**
Lines you draw with the pen do not become part of the slide show.

6. Type **B** to blacken the slide, type **B** to view the slide, type **W** to whiten the slide, press any key, right-click the **slide**, then click **End Show**

 close Annie3.ppt

Figure 7-3: Speaker Notes dialog box

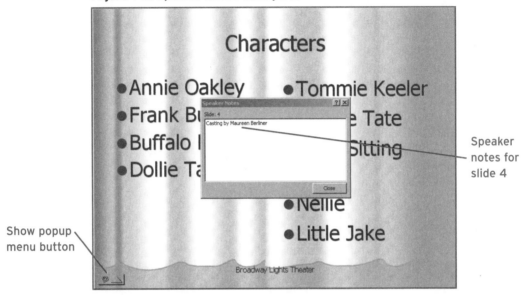

Speaker notes for slide 4

Show popup menu button

Figure 7-4: Meeting Minder dialog box

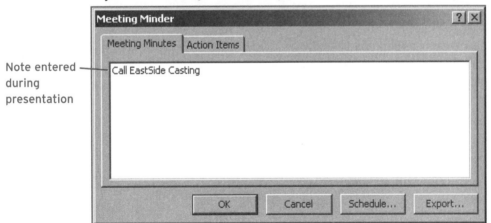

Note entered during presentation

Skill Set 7

Managing and Delivering Presentations

Deliver Presentations

Setup a Custom Show

Often, you will need to deliver a presentation about a particular topic to several different audiences. For instance, you might wish to give a presentation on a particular project not only to a group of employees, but also to prospective clients and existing customers. Each audience will have slightly different interests, and you might want to show each audience only slides relevant to its needs. Fortunately, PowerPoint lets you do all your work in one presentation and then modify it for different audiences by creating a custom show. When you create a custom show, you first choose the slides you want, then give this selection a name. To run a custom show, you open the Custom Shows dialog box, then choose the custom show you want from the list.

Activity Steps

 open Annie4.ppt

1. Click **Slide Show** on the menu bar, click **Custom Shows**, then click **New** in the Custom Shows dialog box

2. Type **Singers** in the Slide show name box in the Define Custom Show dialog box, click **1. Annie Get Your Gun** in the Slides in presentation list, then click **Add** to move it to the Slides in custom show list

3. Add slides 2, 3, 4, 7, 8, 9, and 10 to create a custom show with 8 slides
   See Figure 7-5.

4. Click **OK**
   The custom show named Singers appears in the Custom Shows dialog box.

5. Click **Show** to view the entire Singers custom show

6. Click anywhere to exit the show and return to Slide Sorter view

 close Annie4.ppt

Click the up or down arrow buttons to reorder the slides in the Custom Show dialog box.

Figure 7-5: Defining a custom show

Lists slides in the presentation that are available for the custom show

Name of custom show

Click to reorganize slides in the custom show

Lists slides in custom show

extra!

Adding narrations

If you set your presentation to run automatically—without the benefit of your being there to deliver it—you might want to add voice narration that plays while the slides advance. To record your narration, you need a computer equipped with a microphone and sound card. Select the slide during which you want the narration to begin, click Slide Show on the menu bar, then click Record Narration. Set the microphone level, then click OK to embed the narration. **Embedding** the narration means that the sound files become part of the presentation and travel with it. If you want to minimize the size of your presentation file, you can link the narration instead. **Linking** stores the narration in a separate file in a location you specify. To link your narration to your presentation, click the link check box in the Record Narration dialog box, then specify a location for your narration sound file. If your presentation has a recorded narration and you want to run the show without it, click the Show without narration check box in the Set Up Show dialog box.

Skill Set 7

Managing and Delivering Presentations

Deliver Presentations
Use Onscreen Navigation Tools

When you give a presentation, you might need to locate and show a slide out of sequence. The Go by Title command and the Slide Navigator, both available on the Show Popup menu, let you quickly jump to any slide in your presentation. To open the Show popup menu, right click the screen or click the Show Popup menu button in the lower left corner of the slide. The Show popup menu also provides you with other helpful navigation tools. You can use it to go to the next or previous slide, select a custom show to run, make the screen go black, or end the show at any time.

Activity Steps

 open Annie5.ppt

1. Start the slide show, press **[Spacebar]** to advance to the **Rehearsal Schedule** slide, right-click the **slide** to open the Show popup menu, point to **Go**, then point to **By Title**
   See Figure 7-6.

2. Click **9. Act I song list**

3. Right-click the **Act I song list slide**, point to **Go**, point to **Custom Show**, click **Actors** to begin the Actors custom show, right-click the **Annie Get Your Gun** slide, click **Next,** right-click the **Overview slide**, point to **Go**, then click **Slide Navigator**
   See Figure 7-7.

4. Click **Story** in the Slide Navigator, then click **Go To** to display the Story slide

5. Press **[Esc]** to end the custom show and return to Slide Sorter view

 close Annie5.ppt

Step 5
To view a list of shortcut keys that can help you perform many tasks during a slide show, right-click any slide, then click Help.

Figure 7-6: **Navigation options during a slide show**

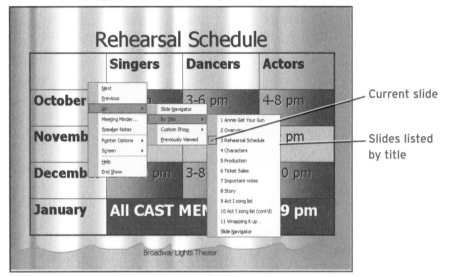

Figure 7-7: **Slide Navigator**

Skill Set 7
Managing and Delivering Presentations

Manage Files and Folders for Presentations
Create Folders for Storing Presentations

When buying real estate, the mantra is "location, location, location." When working with presentations and creating files, the mantra is "organization, organization, organization." If you create folders on your computer that are set up in an organized way and save all your presentation files to these folders, you will be able to find your presentations quickly and easily. If your folders have logical names, whether by client, date, or purpose, you will not lose your files. If your files are systematically named, you won't copy older versions over newer ones, show outdated or incorrect presentations, or find yourself spending precious time trying to locate a particular file. You can create new folders from within PowerPoint using the Save As dialog box. You can also create new folders using My Computer or Windows Explorer.

Step 2
Click History in the Save As dialog box to see a list of all recently opened PowerPoint presentations.

Activity Steps

 open Annie6.ppt

1. Click **File** on the menu bar, then click **Save As** to open the Save As dialog box
   See Figure 7-8.

2. Click the **Create New Folder button** on the Save As dialog box toolbar, type **Annie Get Your Gun** in the Name box in the New Folder dialog box, then click **OK**
   The new folder is a subfolder of the current drive and folder. The Save in box shows the new folder name, and the Save As dialog box displays the contents of the new folder.

3. Type **NewAnnie6** in the File name box, then click **Save** to save the renamed file to the new **Annie Get Your Gun** folder

 close NewAnnie6.ppt

Figure 7-8: Save As dialog box

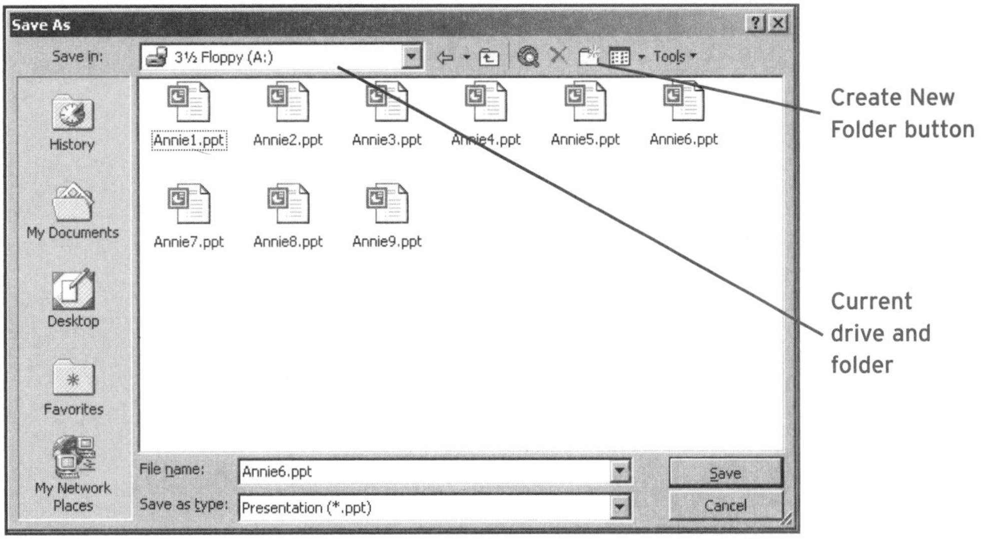

Create New Folder button

Current drive and folder

extra!

Understanding the My Documents folder

The My Documents folder is simply a default folder provided by Windows to help you organize your files. Windows includes shortcuts to this folder in the Save and Open dialog boxes of many applications to help you navigate there quickly. You should consider creating subfolders within My Documents to meet your file management needs. To change the way your files are displayed in the Save As dialog box, click the View button list arrow to select from Large Icons, Small Icons, List, Details, Properties, Preview, Thumbnails, or WebView views.

Skill Set 7
Managing and Delivering Presentations

Work with Embedded Fonts
Embed Fonts in Presentations

If you plan to show your presentation on another computer or have someone else show the presentation for you, you need to make sure that all the fonts you used travel with your file. If your presentation contains unusual fonts, they might not be installed on the computer used to deliver your presentation, and therefore won't appear in your slides. To make sure that all fonts used in your presentation travel with the file, you need to embed the fonts. **Embedding fonts** means including the font file that defines the fonts directly in the presentation file. You can choose to embed only the characters that you used in the presentation or the entire set. To embed fonts with your presentation, you use the Save tab of the Options dialog box, which is available from the Tools menu within PowerPoint or from the Tools menu in the Save As dialog box.

Activity Steps

 open Annie7.ppt

Too many fonts in a presentation can make it look busy and detract from your message. You should limit the number of fonts in any presentation to two or three.

1. Press [F5], then press [Enter] as needed to view the slide show and observe the fonts
   This presentation includes several special fonts such as Lucida Handwriting, Rockwell, Rockwell Extra Bold, ShowCard Gothic, and Broadway.

2. Click **Tools** on the menu bar, click **Options**, then click the **Save tab**

3. Click the **Embed TrueType fonts** check box
   See Figure 7-9.

4. Click **OK**
   When you save the file, the fonts will be saved along with it so you can continue to work on the presentation using all these fonts on any computer.

 close Annie7.ppt

Figure 7-9: Save tab of the Options dialog box

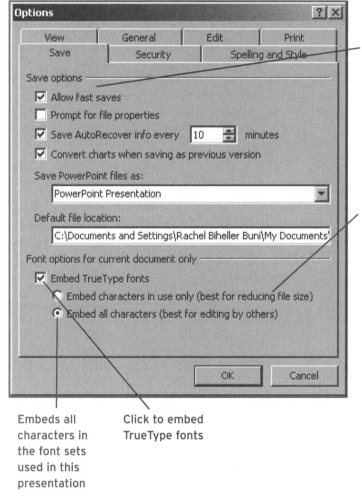

Save options

Only embeds those characters used in this presentation

Embeds all characters in the font sets used in this presentation

Click to embed TrueType fonts

Skill Set 7

Managing and Delivering Presentations

Publish Presentations to the Web
Saving a Presentation as an HTML file

In order to make your presentation available to users on the Internet (known as **publishing** your presentation), you have to save the file as a Web page. Before files can be viewed in a **browser**, the special software used to view Web pages, they must be saved in **Hypertext Markup Language (HTML)**. To save a presentation as a Web page, you use the **Save As Web Page** command on the File menu to open the Save As dialog box, specify a name for the file, and then specify Web Page in the Files of type box to save the file with an .htm extension. PowerPoint creates a folder from the filename and places all the graphics and other required files in it. When you view the presentation as a Web page, each slide title appears on the left side of the browser as a link to a slide. Click the slide titles to view each slide as a Web page. When you save a presentation as a **Web Archive** you create one file that contains all the files required to display Web pages. Web archives can be sent via e-mail and are more easily transported between computers. Older browsers do not support this format.

Activity Steps
 open Annie8.ppt

Click File on the menu bar, then click Properties to view or change the properties of any file, including the title, subject, author, manager, company, keywords, and comments.

1. Click **File** on the menu bar, click **Save as Web Page**, then click **Change Title**
   The Page Title, which will appear in the title bar of a Web page when you view the page in a browser, is determined by the Title name entered in the Properties for the presentation.

2. Type **Annie Get Your Gun** as shown in Figure 7-10, click **OK** to change the page title, click in the **File name box**, select **Annie8**, type **blt-agyg**, then click **Save**
   This filename blt-agyg is used to create the folder to contain all the required files and graphics for the Web pages in that folder.

3. Click **File** on the menu bar, then click **Web Page Preview**
   The presentation displays as Web pages in the default browser for your computer. *See Figure 7-11.*

4. Click **Rehearsal Schedule** in the Navigation frame, click **Story** in the Navigation frame, click **File** on the browser menu bar, then click **Close**

5. Click **File** on the menu bar, click **Save As**, click the **Save as type list arrow**, click **Web Archive (*.mht; *.mhtl)**, click **Save**, then click **Yes** if asked about special characters displaying in some browsers

 close Annie8.ppt

Figure 7-10: Saving a presentation as a Web page and setting the page title

Type Page title here

Filename will be the folder name for required files

Save as an htm or html file

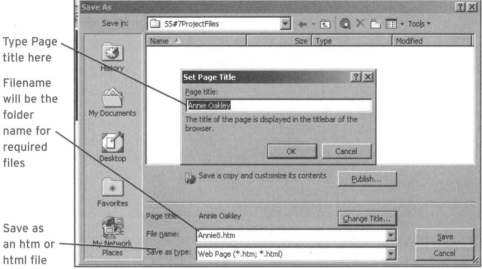

Figure 7-11: Presentation as a Web page in a browser

Internet Explorer browser

Page title

Link pointer

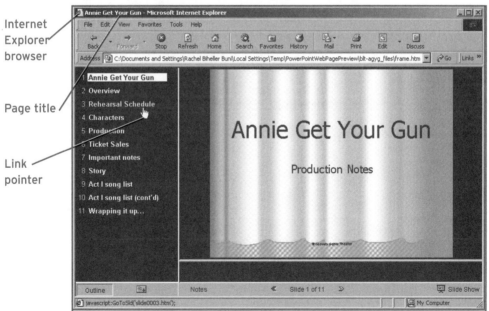

Skill Set 7

Managing and Delivering Presentations

Use Pack and Go
Prepare Presentations for Remote Delivery Using Pack and Go

You don't always have to be there to deliver the presentation in person. However, you do want the presentation to run smoothly whether you are there or not. The Pack and Go Wizard creates a neat package that includes all the required files to run your presentation on any remote computer. You can pack your presentation to a floppy disk, to your hard disk, or across a network to another computer. When you run the Pack and Go wizard, you need to decide whether or not to embed the fonts or to include the **PowerPoint Viewer**, a special program that will run the slide show even if PowerPoint is not installed. Pack and Go creates two files: Preso.ppz and Pngsetup.exe, which are used to unpack and show the presentation.

Step 1
If you get a "This feature is not currently installed..." message, click Yes, then follow the onscreen instructions to navigate to the packandgo folder in the Pack and Go Setup dialog box, then click OK. You will need your Office XP CD to install this feature.

Activity Steps

 open Annie9.ppt

1. Click **File** on the menu bar, click **Pack and Go** to start the Pack and Go Wizard, then click **Next**

2. Verify that the **Active presentation check box** has a check mark, then click **Next**

3. Place a blank formatted floppy disk in Drive A, verify that the **A:\drive option button** is selected, then click **Next**
   See Figure 7-12.

4. Click the **Embed TrueType fonts** check box, verify that the **Include linked files check box** has a check mark, then click **Next**

5. Click **Next** to specify not to include the Viewer, then click **Finish**
   The Pack and Go Status window will tell you how the process is progressing.

6. Click **File** on the menu bar, click **Exit**, double-click **My Computer** on the desktop, navigate to a folder where you can create a new folder, create a new folder called **PackandGoFiles**, navigate to the A: drive, then double-click **Pngsetup.exe**

7. Navigate to the **PackandGoFiles folder** in the Pack and Go Setup dialog box, click **OK**, then click **Yes** to run the presentation

 close Annie9.ppt

Figure 7-12: Pack and Go Wizard

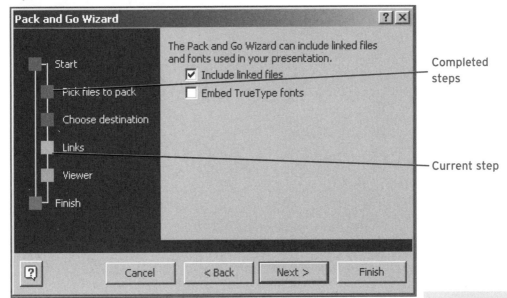

Completed steps

Current step

Skill Set 7

Managing and Delivering Presentations

Target Your Skills

 open Develop1.ppt

1 Use Figure 7-13 as a guide. Specify the show type as a presentation given by a speaker on a full screen, set the show to loop continuously until Escape, and set the pen color to red. Embed the TrueType fonts (only the characters in use.) Open the Meeting Minder, then type your name at the end of the notes.

 open Jewels1.ppt

2 Use Figure 7-14 as a guide. Save the presentation as a Web page Jewels.htm. Embed the fonts in the file. Use the navigation frame to click the links for all six slides. Save the file as a Web archive. Use the Pack and Go Wizard. Unpack and view the presentation file.

Figure 7-13

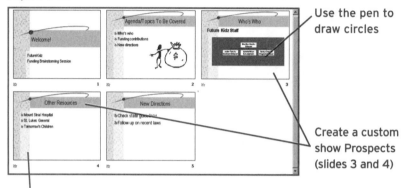

Use the pen to draw circles

Create a custom show Prospects (slides 3 and 4)

While the slide show is running, add speaker notes "Contact Michael Dumont at HUMDC"

Figure 7-14

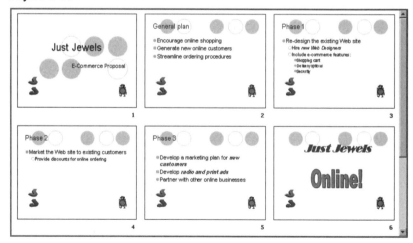

Skill List

1. Set up a review cycle
2. Review presentation comments
3. Schedule and deliver presentation broadcasts
4. Publish presentations to the Web

Collaborating on team-based projects lets you combine everyone's best skills to achieve a shared goal. PowerPoint provides powerful collaboration tools to facilitate working in groups. If you are creating a presentation with colleagues, or just want input from others on a presentation you are creating by yourself, you can easily get feedback by setting up a review cycle. A **review cycle** is the process of routing a file to specified reviewers, where each reviewer's comments are added to the file. You can send a presentation via e-mail or across a network to colleagues for review. If more than one person is working on the team, the first reviewer can enter any changes or comments into the presentation and then pass it to the next reviewer. All additional reviewer comments and changes are added to the file along with information about each review pass. Once all colleagues have seen and reviewed the file and the review cycle is complete, you can review, accept, or reject the contributions of your colleagues.

When you deliver a presentation, you and your audience do not have to be in the same room. You can schedule and deliver online broadcasts for viewing over an **intranet**, a network of interlinked computers that is restricted to a specific company or group of people. During the broadcast, you can use PowerPoint's tools to interact with your audience and gather feedback from them. You can also publish the presentation to a Web server so that the slide show can be viewed by anyone at any time on the Web.

Skill Set 8

Set Up a Review Cycle
Set Up a Review Cycle and Send Presentations for Review

To set up a review cycle you need to send the file using your e-mail program. The steps in this activity assume you will use Outlook 2002. If you use another e-mail program, Outlook will still manage the review cycle for you. To send the file to more than one reviewer, use the **Send To Routing Recipient** command to open the Add Routing Slip dialog box. This lets you choose the addresses of the recipients and specify options, such as whether all recipients receive the file all at once, or one after the other so that each reviewer can see the previous reviewers' comments. A **routing slip** travels with the file and contains the e-mail addresses of the people who are on the list to receive the file. If a file has a routing slip attached to it, each reviewer has the chance to add a new address to the slip or just send the presentation to the next person on the list.

Activity Steps

 open BLT-Season1.ppt

1. Click **File** on the menu bar, point to **Send To**, then click **Routing Recipient** (if a dialog box opens asking you to allow access to addresses stored in Outlook, click **Yes**)

2. If the Choose Profile dialog box opens, select your **profile name**, then click **OK**
   The Add Routing Slip dialog box opens. *See Figure 8-1.*

Step 2 and 3

If a warning dialog box opens telling you that a program is trying to access e-mail addresses stored in Outlook, click Yes.

3. Click **Address** to open your Outlook address book (if you are using another e-mail program, the address book for that e-mail program will open)

4. Choose the names of two people to whom you want to send the file, click **OK** to return to the Add Routing Slip dialog box, then verify that the **One after another option button** is selected in the Route to recipients section

5. Click **Route**, click **Yes** to access the e-mail addresses if the warning dialog box opens, then click **Yes** to send the e-mail
   The file is sent to the first recipient.

6. Click **File** on the menu bar, point to **Send To**, then click **Mail Recipient (for Review)**
   The Outlook new message window opens. *See Figure 8-2.* To send the file for review, you would fill in the recipients' e mail addresses, then click Send.

7. Click **File** on the new message window menu bar, click **Close**, then click **No** to return to PowerPoint

 close BLT-Season1.ppt

Figure 8-1: Add Routing Slip dialog box

Lists all addresses in route

Click to select addresses from Contacts file

Click to choose whether file is sent in a loop or to all recipients at once

Figure 8-2: Message window in Outlook

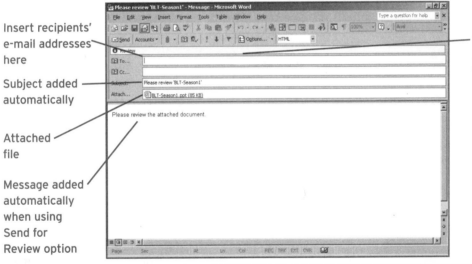

Insert recipients' e-mail addresses here

Subject added automatically

Attached file

Message added automatically when using Send for Review option

Banner indicates file is attached for review

extra!

Understanding different sending options

If you want to send the presentation to only one person, you can use the **Send To Mail Recipient (as Attachment)** command to attach the file to an e-mail message, so a recipient can open, view, and edit it. If you want a message to be included automatically in the e-mail requesting that the recipient review the attachment, you can use the **Send To Mail Recipient (for Review)** command. To make changes to the routing of a file, click File on the menu bar, point to Send To, then click Routing Recipient to open the Edit Routing Slip dialog box. This lets you change the order of recipients, add recipients, or change the routing for the file.

Skill Set 8
Workgroup Collaboration

Review Presentation Comments
Reviewing, Acccepting, and Rejecting Changes from Multiple Reviewers

If you send your presentation to more than one reviewer, you will get back several versions of the presentation with comments and tracked changes. Depending on the options specified by the original sender, the file will go to all recipients at once, or in sequence. The status of the file may or may not be tracked to allow the originator to see the progress. Fortunately, you can merge all the files so that you can review all the comments at once and accept or reject any of the changes. When the file arrives in your e-mail, you have the option of merging it with your original file or opening it for review as shown in Figure 8-3. Each reviewer's comments appear in a different color, tagged with the date of the comment and the reviewer's initials or name.

Each reviewer is assigned a different color to make it easy to distinguish among reviewers. To view a list of all the reviewers who have contributed to the file, click the Reviewers list arrow in the revisions pane.

Activity Steps

 open BLT-Season2.ppt

1. Click **Tools** on the menu bar, then click **Compare and Merge Presentations**
   The Choose Files to Merge with Current Presentation dialog box opens.

2. Click **BLT-Season2-rev.ppt**, click **Merge**, click **Continue**, then click **Next** in the Revisions Pane to go to Slide 2

3. Place the pointer over the **ECB1 colored box** on the slide to read the comment
   See Figure 8-4.

4. Click **Next** in the revisions pane to move to slide 3, view the comment, click **Next** to move to slide 4, then click **Text 2: Established in 1987** in the Revisions Pane to open a popup window listing the suggested changes
   See Figure 8-5. You can use the Reviewing toolbar or the Revisions Pane to apply suggested changes.

5. Click in the **Inserted paragraph separator check box** in the popup window to see the first change, then click the **Inserted "In 2004..." check box**

6. Click **Next** in the Revisions Pane, click **Text 2: 50% from ticket sales...**, click the **Apply button** to view all the suggested slide changes, then click the **Unapply button** to reject the changes

7. Click **Next** in the Revisions Pane, click **Text 2: Elementary programs...**, add check marks to each check box, view the changes, click **Next**, then view and apply the change to slide 11

 close BLT-Season2.ppt

Figure 8-3: Message dialog box to determine whether to merge or open file

Figure 8-4: Reviewing a comment

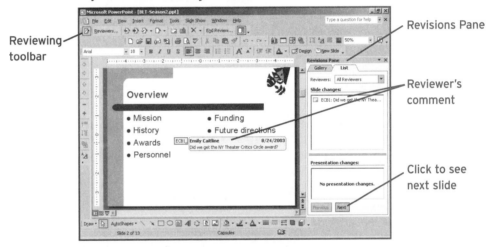

Reviewing toolbar

Revisions Pane

Reviewer's comment

Click to see next slide

Figure 8-5: Comments in revisions pane

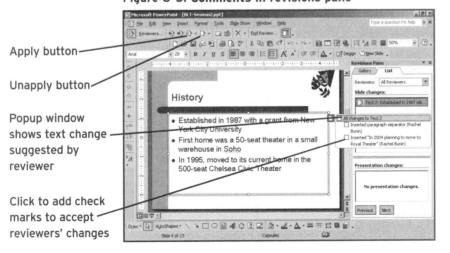

Apply button

Unapply button

Popup window shows text change suggested by reviewer

Click to add check marks to accept reviewers' changes

To delete a comment, click the comment on the slide, then click the Delete Comment button on the Reviewing toolbar.

Skill Set 8

Workgroup Collaboration

Schedule and Deliver Presentation Broadcasts
Set Up and Schedule Online Broadcasts

You can deliver a presentation over the Web, on the Internet, or over a network as an online broadcast. An **Online broadcast** is a live performance of your presentation that is captured and delivered over the Web or a network to viewers through a browser. Your audience must use Netscape Navigator 4.0 (or later) or Internet Explorer 5.1 (or later) to view an online broadcast. You also must have access to a shared network drive or a URL to be able to schedule an online broadcast.

When you set up an online broadcast, PowerPoint creates a **lobby page**, which contains information about the title, subject, host name, and time of the broadcast and appears in the viewer's browser before the broadcast begins.

Activity Steps

 open BLT-Season3.ppt

1. Click **Slide Show** on the menu bar, point to **Online Broadcast**, then click **Schedule a Live Broadcast**

2. Type the information in the Title and Description box in the Schedule Presentation Broadcast dialog box shown in Figure 8-6
   The information will appear in the lobby page.

3. Click **Settings**, click **Browse** on the Presenter tab, then navigate to the location of the shared folder to save the broadcast
   The File location must be a shared folder on a network server or a URL for a broadcast on the Web.

4. If you don't have a shared folder, click **OK** to close the error box, then click **Cancel** in the Broadcast Settings dialog box

5. If you are able to specify a shared folder on a network in the Broadcast Settings dialog box, click **OK**, then click **Schedule**
   If you have a shared network folder and Outlook, the program will open a meeting request window. *See Figure 8-7.*

6. Close the Meeting window if one is open, do not save the changes, then click **Cancel** in the Schedule a Presentation Broadcast window

7. To broadcast the show at the scheduled time, click **Slide Show** on the menu bar, point to **Online Broadcast**, click **Start a Live Broadcast Now** (if you have Outlook, click **Yes** to allow access) to open the Live Presentation Broadcast dialog box

8. Click **Cancel**

 close BLT-Season3.ppt

If you get a dialog box that says the Online Broadcast feature isn't currently installed, click Install then follow the onscreen steps to install the feature.

Figure 8-6: Schedule Presentation Broadcast dialog box

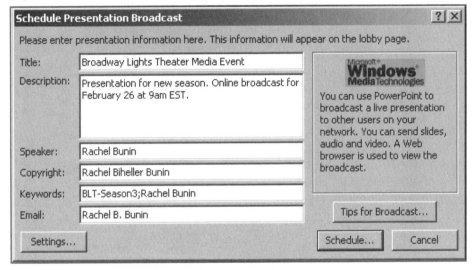

Figure 8-7: Meeting request window in Outlook

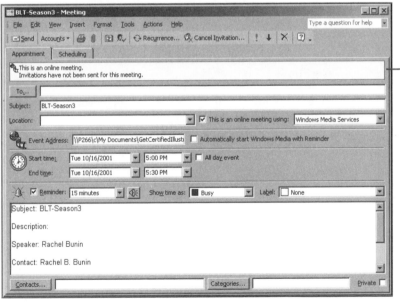

Fill in these boxes to specify the time and attendees for your presentation

extra!

Sharing folders

If you are working on a network, you can specify a folder as shared by right-clicking the folder in the Windows Explorer window, clicking Sharing, then clicking the share this folder option button.

Skill Set 8

Workgroup Collaboration

Publish Presentations to the Web
Save Presentations as Web Pages (Using the Publish Option)

If you want to allow others to view your presentation whenever they want, you can save the presentation as a Web page and publish it to the Web. **Publishing** a Web page means that you place it on a Web server so that users can view it through a browser any time they find convenient. This differs from an online broadcast, which you, the presenter, schedule for a specific time. To publish a presentation to the Web, you must first save it as a Web page in HTML Format. Once it is saved as a Web page, you can use the Publish option in the Save As dialog box to specify the location of your Web server. Once a file is published to a Web server, it is available to anyone with Internet access.

Activity Steps

 open BLT-Season4.ppt

1. Click **File** on the menu bar, then click **Save As Web Page** to open the Save as dialog box.
   See Figure 8-8.

2. Navigate to the folder containing your Project Files, click **Change Title**, type **your name**, click **OK**, then click **Publish**
   The Publish as Web Page dialog box opens. *See Figure 8-9.*

3. Click the **Open published Web page in browser check box**, then click **Publish**
   The presentation opens in your default browser. Unless you specified a Web server location in the Publish as Web Page dialog box, the file will not be available on the Web to other viewers.

4. Click each link to view all 13 slides, click **File** on the browser menu bar, then click **Close** to return to PowerPoint

 close BLT-Season4.ppt

The Web page title appears in the title bar of each page.

Figure 8-8: Save As dialog box

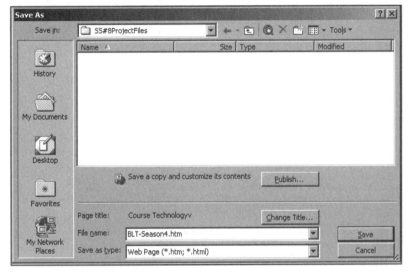

Figure 8-9: Publish as Web Page dialog box

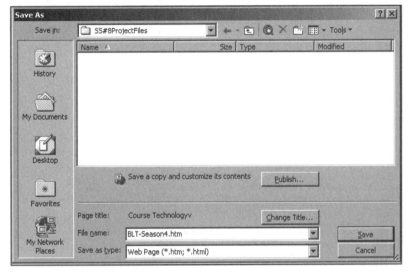

Click to open the presentation in a browser

extra!

Using the Publish option

When you click the Publish button, PowerPoint creates a folder within the drive and folder you specify in the Publish as Web Page dialog box to store all the required files. The presentation is saved as an htm file in the folder you specify. If the drive you specify is a Web server, these files will be available on the Web. When you publish a presentation file, a navigation frame is created for each slide that is identified by the slide title.

Skill Set 8

Workgroup Collaboration

Target Your Skills

 open Shelter1.ppt

1 With Figure 8-10 as a guide, send the file Shelter1.ppt for review to two friends using the Send to Routing Recipient command. Compare and merge the Shelter1.ppt file with the file Shelter1-rev.ppt. Reject the change to add Angela on slide 5. Accept all the other changes to the presentation. Delete the comment on slide 4.

 open Shelter2.ppt

2 Use Figure 8-11 as a guide. Save the presentation as a Web page and use the Publish option to publish the presentation to a location on your hard drive. Change the title to your name. If you have access to a shared network folder or URL on a Web site, schedule an online broadcast for the presentation.

Figure 8-10

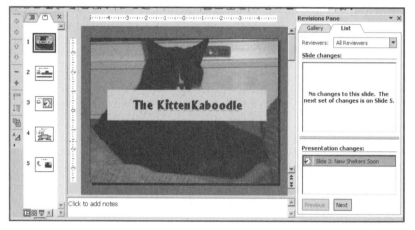

Figure 8-11

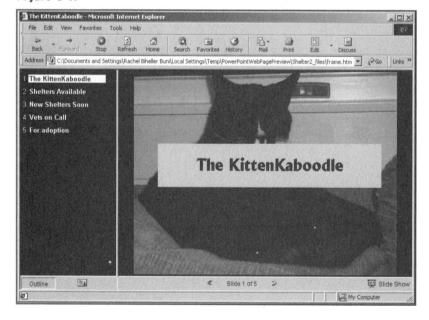

Projects List

Project 1 – Geranium Bistro Business Plan Presentation

Project 2 – Tips for Home Security Presentation

Project 3 – Orientation Presentation for Camp Dream Quest

Project 4 – Great Cathedrals of Europe Tour Presentation

Project 5 – "How to Draw People" Instructional Presentation

Project 6 – Sales Presentation for Road Smart Driving School

Project 7 – Lecture Presentation for E-Commerce Marketing

Project 8 – Rainforest Coalition Web Pages

The PowerPoint MOUS skill sets include the features and functions you need to create, modify, and deliver presentations. In the following projects, you will develop and modify various presentations by inserting and modifying visual elements such as tables, charts, and clip art. You will also explore different presentation delivery options such as transition and animation effects, and enhance a presentation with data from other sources, including Excel charts, Word tables, and sound and video files. Finally, you will work with options designed to facilitate collaboration between two or more people working on the same presentation.

Project for Skill Set 1

Creating Presentations

Geranium Bistro Business Plan Presentation

You've just started working for the Geranium Bistro, a family-style café overlooking a lake in rural Minnesota. The owner would like to obtain financing to expand the café to better serve a large clientele of summer visitors. He asks you to create the outline of a presentation that he can use to describe his business plan to investors. You will start by checking out the Business Plan AutoContent wizard, and then you will create a new presentation containing titles for six slides.

Activity Steps

1. Start PowerPoint, then use the AutoContent wizard to create an onscreen presentation using the Business Plan template; enter **Geranium Bistro** as the Presentation title and **2004 Business Plan** in the footer, along with the default footer options

2. Scroll through the completed presentation to get a feel for its contents, then close the new presentation without saving it
   Now that you have an idea of the contents of a typical business plan presentation, you're ready to create your own version.

3. Create a new blank presentation, apply the **Profile slide design**, then close the Slide Design task pane

4. In the Outline tab, add **five** slides to the presentation for a total of six slides, then enter the text shown in Figure PP 1-1

5. In the presentation footer, add **your name**, the **current date** in the format that corresponds to **July 17, 2004** that updates automatically, and the **slide number**; do not include the footer on the title slide

6. Delete **Slide 3** from the presentation

7. Save the presentation as **PC_Project1.ppt**

8. Compare **Slide 1** to Figure PP 1-2

 close PC_Project1.ppt

Figure PP 1-1: Slide titles for Geranium Bistro Business Plan presentation

Figure PP 1-2: Slide 1 of Business Plan presentation

Project for Skill Set 2

Inserting and Modifying Text

Tips for Home Security Presentation

Great Western Security needs to develop a presentation to be delivered to residents of a local condominium complex who are interested in installing a home security system. Most of the content for the presentation is already contained in a Word outline. In this project, you will open the Word outline in PowerPoint, edit selected slides, and add text to some new slides.

Activity Steps

1. Start PowerPoint, then insert the Word outline from the file **PC_Project2.doc** into a blank presentation

2. Delete the first slide in the presentation, apply the **Title slide layout** to the new **Slide 1**, then close the Slide Layout task pane

3. Change the font of the title text to **Arial Black**, then apply Italics to the subtitle text

4. On **Slide 4**, delete the word **personal**, then insert the word **security** before "system"

5. On **Slide 5**, add a bullet with the text **Sign the contract and provide a check for the first and last month's payment**, as shown in Figure PP 2-1

6. Apply the **Blends** slide design to the entire presentation then close the Slide Design task pane

7. View the presentation in Slide Sorter view
   The presentation appears in Slide Sorter view as shown in Figure PP 2-2.

 close PC_Project2.ppt

Figure PP 2-1: Modified Slide 5

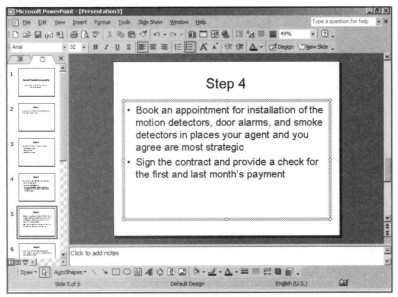

Figure PP 2-2: Home Security presentation in Slide Sorter view

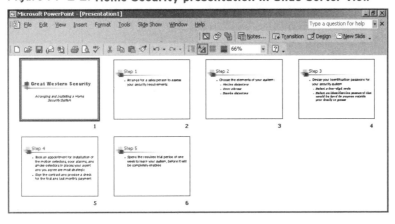

Project for Skill Set 3

Inserting and Modifying Visual Elements

Orientation Presentation for Camp Dream Quest

Camp Dream Quest in Costa Rica provides teens from all over the world with a three-week program of outdoor adventure activities, including hiking and camping in the rainforest and snorkeling, swimming, and sailing in the warm Pacific waters off the Costa Rican coast. The camp administration has prepared a PowerPoint presentation to deliver to school groups throughout the US and Canada. In this project, you will enhance the presentation with graphical elements that include a table, charts, clip art, bitmap images, and drawn objects. The six slides of the completed presentation appear as shown in Figure PP 3-1.

Activity Steps

 open PC_Project3.ppt

1. In Slide Master view, insert the picture file **Hibiscus.jpg** so that it appears in the top right corner of every slide in the presentation, except the first slide

2. Size and position the hibiscus picture as shown in Figure PP 3-1

3. Open the Clip Gallery, search for **Costa Rica**, then insert, size, and position the clip art image of a flag on **Slide 1**, as shown in Figure PP 3-1

4. On **Slide 3**, draw a **sun shape**, fill the shape with the **Papyrus texture** and remove the border line, then size and position the shape as shown in Figure PP 3-1

5. On **Slide 4**, insert the picture file **Turtle.jpg**, then size and position the picture as shown in Figure PP 3-1

6. On **Slide 4**, insert a text box to the left of the turtle picture, as shown in Figure PP 3-1, enter the text **Meet Tio, our school turtle!** in the text box then enhance it with 40-pt

7. On **Slide 5**, insert a chart using the information shown below, change the chart type to **pie**, change the font color of the chart legend text to black, then remove the border around the pie chart

    16 17 18 19
    25 40 75 60

8. On **Slide 6**, create the table and enter the text shown in Figure PP 3-1

9. Modify the table by reducing its height and width, filling it with light yellow, changing the font color to black, removing the Shadow effect, then changing the border lines to black

 close PC_Project3.ppt

Step 5
Note that you must be connected to the Internet to insert this piece of clip art from the complete Microsoft Clip Gallery.

Figure PP 3-1: Completed presentation for Camp Dream Quest

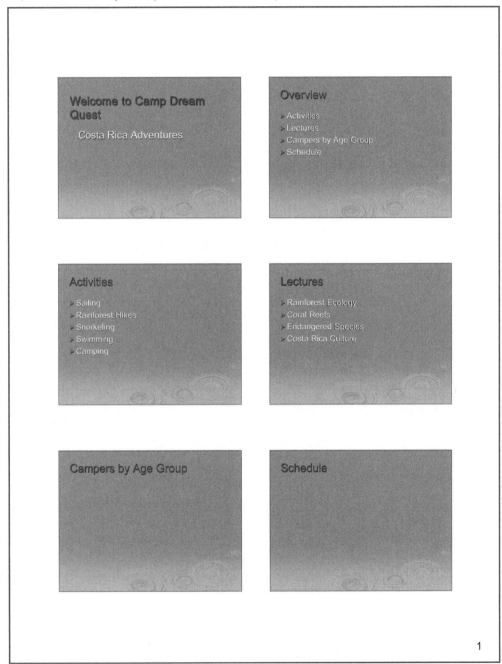

Project for Skill Set 4

Modifying Presentation Format

Great Cathedrals of Europe Tour Presentation

Creative Tours, Inc. puts together customized tours of Europe and Asia for small special interest groups. You have been asked to enhance a presentation that describes a tour of six cathedrals. In this project, you will apply formats to the presentation, apply animation schemes and transition effects, customize slide formats, templates, and the slide master, and then add links to the presentation. Figure PP 4-1 shows the 9 slides in the completed presentation.

Activity Steps

 open PC_Project4.ppt

1. Change **Slide 1** of the presentation so that its background color is a **very light blue**

2. Modify the design template by removing the graphic that appears along the right side of every slide and then apply **bold** to the **title text** on both the slide master and the title slide master

3. In Slide Sorter view, apply the **Watermark** design template to **Slides 5** and **6**, apply the **Pixel** design template to **Slides 7** and **8**, then select the color scheme for the Pixel design template that shows chart elements in **red tones**

4. Apply the **Float** animation scheme to **Slide 1**, then apply the **Zoom** animation scheme to the remaining slides

5. Apply the **Wheel Clockwise, 8 Spokes** transition effect to the last slide in the presentation, then apply the **Shape Diamond** transition effect to **Slides 1** through **8** of the presentation

6. Delete the Slide Master called **Light Text Master**, create a new Slide Master called **Yellow Slide Master** that includes a light yellow background, then apply the Yellow Slide Master to **Slides 2** and **9** in the presentation

7. Move the two slides for **Germany** before the two slides for **France**, then apply the **Title and Text slide layout** to Slide 3 (Cologne Cathedral)

8. On **Slide 2**, make each country name a hyperlink to the first of its related slides

9. Set the time between each slide at **2 seconds**, then rehearse the timing by running the show in Slide Show view, starting from Slide 1

 close PC_Project4.ppt

Step 2
Remember that you need to work in the Slide Master to delete a graphic from every slide in the presentation.

Figure PP 4-1: Completed presentation for Cathedrals Tour

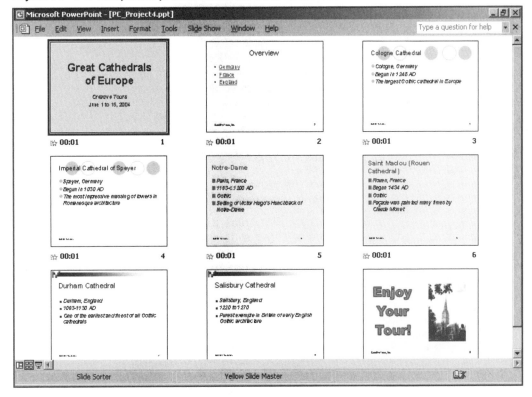

Project for Skill Set 5

Printing Presentations

"How to Draw People" Instructional Presentation

An instructor at a local art school has prepared an instructional presentation to deliver to his portrait class. He asks you to help him print the presentation in various ways. First, you'll print selected slides in black and white, and then you will print the presentation as handouts of three slides per page with space allocated for note-taking. Finally, you'll print the instructor's speaker notes that he plans to refer to while delivering the presentation.

Activity Steps

 open PC_Project5.ppt

1. Preview the presentation, then print **Slides 3** and **4** as pure black and white slides

2. Print the entire presentation as black and white handouts containing three slides per page
   Figure PP 5-1 shows how the first page of the handouts appears. The entire presentation consists of six slides and will print over two pages.

3. In the Notes master, format the speaker notes by changing the font size of the notes to **18 point** and the font to **Times New Roman**

4. Print the speaker notes for **Slides 2** and **3** in Grayscale
   Figure PP 5-2 shows how the speaker notes for Slide 2 appear when printed.

 close PC_Project5.ppt

Figure PP 5-1: Page 1 of the printed presentation

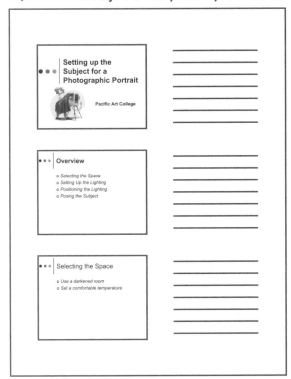

Figure PP 5-2: Notes page for Slide 2

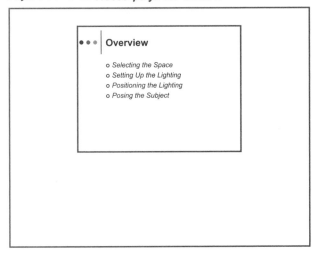

Project for Skill Set 6

Working with Data from Other Sources

Sales Presentation for Road Smart Driving School

Road Smart Driving School in Tulsa, Oklahoma offers four levels of driving courses—from an introductory teen driving course to a commercial driving course. Some of the content for a Road Smart Driving School presentation is contained in Word and Excel files. In this project, you will modify the current presentation by inserting this content, some of which will be linked to source files so that any changes made to the content in the source files also appear in the presentation. You will also insert a sound file and a video file into the presentation. Figure PP 6-1 shows the six slides in the completed presentation.

Activity Steps

 open PC_Project6A.ppt

1. Import the Word file **PC_Project6B.doc** as an embedded object on **Slide 3**, then size and position the table as shown in Figure PP 6-1

2. Start Excel, then open the file **PC_Project6C.xls**, copy the **column chart** and paste it on **Slide 4**, then size and position it as shown in Figure PP 6-1

3. Insert the Excel file **PC_Project6D.xls** as a linked file on **Slide 5**

4. Insert the Word file **PC_Project6E.doc** as a linked file on **Slide 6**

Step 5
To change the media file type in the Insert Clip Art task pane, click the Results should be like list arrow, deselect Clip Art, Photographs, and Movies, then click Search.

5. Insert the sound file **Bulb Horn** in the bottom right corner of Slide 1 by opening the Insert Clip Art task pane, entering the keyword **cars** in the Search text text box, specifying that the results be only **Sounds**, and answering Yes to have the sound played automatically when the slide show is launched

6. In the yellow area on Slide 1, insert the media clip shown in Figure PP 6-1 by searching for **freeway** in the insert Clip Art task pane and specifying that search results should be only **Movies**

7. View the completed presentation in Slide Show view, export the presentation to a Word outline, then save the Word outline as **PC_Project6F.doc**

 close PC_Project6A.ppt   PC_Project6D.doc
PC_Project6B.xls   PC_Project6E.xls
PC_Project6C.doc   PC_Project6F.doc

Figure PP 6-1: Completed presentation for Road Smart Driving School

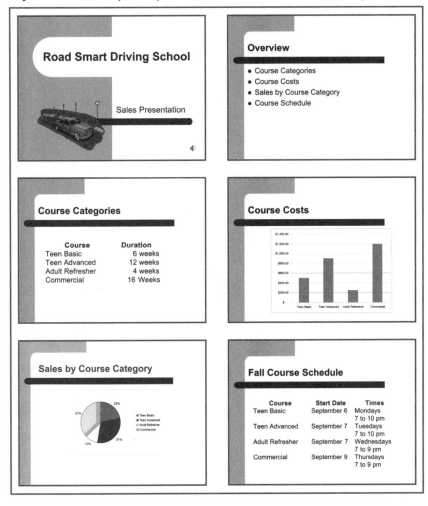

Project for Skill Set 7

Managing and Delivering Presentations

Lecture Presentation for E-Commerce Marketing

You are helping an instructor of a business course in E-Commerce to prepare slides for delivery as part of a lecture. The instructor would like students to view some of the slides in the presentation as a continuous loop on the lab computers. The instructor also wants you to create a folder in which to store the presentation. In addition, the instructor plans to publish the presentation on the World Wide Web for students to review following the in-class lecture. Finally, the instructor plans to deliver the lecture as a self-running presentation from a computer that is not equipped with PowerPoint. Figure PP 7-1 shows the completed presentation.

Activity Steps

 open PC_Project7.ppt

1. Create a new folder called **E-Commerce** on your hard drive or floppy disk, then save the current presentation in this folder

2. Change the pen color to **yellow**, run the slide show, then annotate **Slide 6** of the presentation by drawing an **x** through the **Spam** WordArt object

Step 4
To move from slide to slide while viewing the presentation, right-click the slide displayed in the window, then click Advance on the shortcut menu.

3. Set up the presentation so that **Slides 3** through **7** can be browsed by an individual in a window, be run continuously until Esc is pressed, and advanced manually

4. View slides **3** through **7** of the presentation in Slide Show view

5. Save the presentation as an HTML file called **Marketing.htm**

6. Set up the presentation so that all slides are run continuously at a kiosk at **3 second** intervals, then view the slide show

7. Use **Pack and Go** to prepare the presentation for delivery on a computer that does not have PowerPoint loaded; choose to copy the file to the A: drive and insert a floppy disk when prompted, select both the **Include Linked Files** and **Embed TrueType fonts check boxes**, and do not include a viewer

 close Marketing.htm

Figure PP 7-1: E-Commerce presentation in Slide Sorter view

Project for Skill Set 8

PowerPoint Core Projects

Rainforest Coalition Web Pages

Sally Reisman, an administrator at the British Columbia Rainforest Coalition, has put together two slides in PowerPoint that she would like to publish to the coalition's new Web site. She has collaborated with her colleague, Joe Watson, about the content of the two slides. She creates one version of the slides and sends them to Joe. He inserts some comments and makes some changes and then sends the presentation back to Sally. In this project, you will use collaboration options to review the two versions of the presentation.

Activity Steps

 open PC_Project8A.ppt

1. Read Sally's comment on **Slide 1**, enter the e-mail address **info@rainforestcoalition.com** below the text BC Rainforest Coalition on Slide1, then reduce the font size of the e-mail address to 18-point

2. On **Slide 2**, insert a comment in the **Cougars** text box with the text **How about we use a wolf picture instead?**

3. Save the file, click **Tools** on the menu bar, then click **Compare and Merge Presentations**

4. In the Compare and Merge Presentations dialog box, select **PC_Project8B.ppt**, click **Merge**, then click **Continue**

5. On **Slide 1**, show Joe Watson's changes, then accept the **Inserted "British Columbia"** change and the **Deleted "BC"** change

6. On **Slide 2**, accept Joe's changes, then read and delete his comment

7. Replace **Cougars** with **Wolves**, delete the clip art of the cougar, open the Insert Clip Art task pane, search for **sea wolf**, then insert, size and position the clip art, as shown in Figure PP 8-1

8. Delete all the comments in the presentation, then save the presentation as a Web page

9. In the Save as dialog box, click **Publish** to open the Publish as a Web Page dialog box, click the **Open published Web page in browser check box**, click **Publish**, then maximize the Web browser window

   The presentation appears in the Web browser as shown in Figure PP 8-2.

10. Close the browser

 close PC_Project8A.ppt

Figure PP 8-1: New clip art inserted on Slide 2

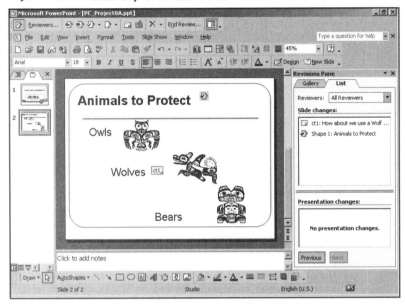

Figure PP 8-2: Presentation displayed in Web browser

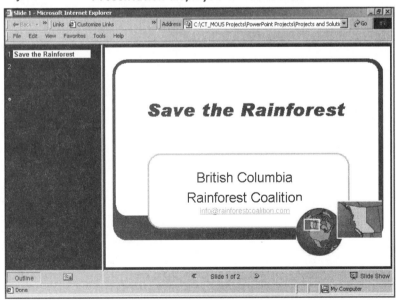

Glossary

Action button A premade button that you can use to create hyperlinks for commonly used activities such as navigating among slides and playing sounds or video.

Animated gif files Files that contain multiple static images that stream to create an animated effect and that have the file extension .gif.

Animation The motion of text and objects on a slide along with special visual and sound effects.

Animation schemes Preset visual effects that you can apply to text on a slide that make the text move in specific ways. Animation schemes are divided into three categories: Subtle, Moderate, and Exciting, to help you choose just the right animation for your presentation and audience.

Ask a Question box A box on the menu bar in which you can type a question to access the Help system to get help on a topic.

Assistant shape Item at a lower hierarchical level in an organization chart that connects to any other shape with an elbow connector.

AutoContent wizard Series of dialog boxes that asks you to choose your presentation purpose and how you plan to present it, and then creates a presentation with sample content and a professional-looking design.

AutoShapes Group of ready-made graphics that come with PowerPoint and include basic shapes such as squares and circles as well as elaborate shapes such as banners and stars.

Background The color or design that appears as a canvas behind the text on a slide which you can change or modify or to which you can apply one of PowerPoint's special effects.

Bitmap image An image stored as a series of small dots. The most common bitmap image file format is .bmp, but others are .jpg, .tif, .png, and .gif.

Browser Special software used to view Web pages, such as Opera, Internet Explorer, and Netscape Navigator.

Categories Data represented along the horizontal or X-axis of a chart.

Cell The basic unit of a table; the intersection of a column and a row.

Chart A graphic presentation of data useful for showing trends or comparisons.

Clip art A collection of ready made images available through the Clip Organizer that you can use to enhance your presentation.

Clip Organizer The repository for storing, organizing, and retrieving clips in Office XP programs.

Clips Media files such as drawings, images, photographs, sounds and video stored in the Clip Organizer for Office XP programs.

Color scheme A set of eight colors that is consistently applied to fonts, accents, hyperlinks, backgrounds, and fills.

Column head The first row of a table, used to identify the content of each column.

Compressing images Reducing the file size of an image. Does not affect the physical measurements of the image.

Coworker shapes Items in an organization chart that show peers within the hierarchy at an equal level to each other.

Custom show PowerPoint feature that lets you customize a single presentation for several different audiences, letting you show only slides that will be relevant to the needs of a particular audience.

Data series The information in a datasheet row that is represented in a chart with a unique color.

Datasheet A table made up of lettered columns and numbered rows, which intersect to form cells, and which provides placeholder text and numbers that you can replace with new data.

Design template A file that contains all the specifications for how a presentation looks, including background designs, color schemes, fonts, and layout.

Destination file The file that contains a linked or embedded object.

Embedded object An object created in one program (such as a worksheet created in Excel) and placed into another (such as PowerPoint. Clicking the embedded object activates the source program so you can make changes to the object using the source program's tools. Changes to the object in the destination file are not reflected in the source file.

Embedding Inserting an object created in another program, called a **source program**, into your presentation. Once you embed an object into a presentation, the object becomes part of the presentation file and no longer has a connection to the **source file**, where the object was originally created, though it does stay connected to the program where it was created.

Embedding fonts Feature that lets you package the font file that defines a particular set of fonts directly in the presentation file so that all the fonts in your presentation can be displayed on any computer.

Excel 2002 The spreadsheet program included with the Microsoft Office XP software.

Fill effects Special effects such as patterns or shading used to enhance a slide background.

Folder A subdivision on a computer's hard disk used to organize files.

Footer Text information, such as the date, the presentation name, your company name, or the slide number, that appears at the bottom of every slide, notes page, or handout.

Handout Master Specifies how the slides will be positioned on the handouts and also lets you change the header and footer.

Handouts Printed copies of your slides containing 1, 2. 3. . or 9 slides per page that you can provide your audience to help them follow the presentation.

Hidden slides Slides that you designated not to show or print for a particular audience.

Hyperlink Text or an object on a slide that you click to connect to another location. In PowerPoint you can add hyperlinks on a slide to connect to another slide in the same presentation, a slide in another presentation, or a Web page on the Internet.

Hypertext Markup Language (HTML) The computer language format for all pages that are viewed through browsers on the World Wide Web.

Intranet A network of interlinked computers that is restricted to a specific company or group of people.

Kiosk A computer used to display information in a remote setting such as a mall or building lobby.

Layout The organization of text and graphics on a slide.

Legend Identifies each data series and its assigned color in the chart, each of which is identified by the labels in the first row and first column of the datasheet.

Linked object An object created in one program (such as a Word table) that is inserted into another program (such as PowerPoint), where the inserted object remains connected to the source file so that any changes made to the object in the source file are reflected in the object in the destination file.

Lobby page Page created by PowerPoint when you set up an online broadcast that serves as an introduction for your audience and contains information about the title, subject, host name, and time of the broadcast. Appears in the viewer's browser before the broadcast begins.

Meeting Minder Feature that lets you keep track of meeting minutes, or record action items while the slide show is running.

Menu bar Bar located below the title bar in the PowerPoint window that contains the menus for accessing PowerPoint commands. You click a menu to open it.

Normal view The view where you create and modify slides, and which has four work areas: the **Outline tab**, the **slides tab**, the **Slide pane** and the **Notes pane**.

Notes pages Printed pages that contain a copy of the slides along with presenter notes on what to say about each slide.

Notes pane In Normal view, the area below the Slide pane where you type notes for the presentation. Notes appear on the Notes pages.

Online broadcast A live performance of your presentation that is captured and delivered over the Web or a network to viewers through a browser.

Organization charts Graphic diagram used to show the hierarchy of employees in a business or relationships of things or people to each other. Often called **org charts.**

Outline tab In Normal view, the tab that displays all the text that is in text and title placeholders in a presentation.

Pack and Go Wizard Creates a neat package that includes all the required files to run your presentation on any remote computer. You can pack your presentation to a floppy disk, to your hard disk, or across a network to another computer.

Page numbers Slide numbers on printed notes pages and handouts that are contained in the header or footer.

PowerPoint Viewer A special program that makes it possible to run a PowerPoint slide show even if PowerPoint is not installed

PowerPoint 2002 The presentation graphics program that is part of the Microsoft Office XP suite.

Presentation A PowerPoint file, that has a .ppt file extension.

Presentation window Work area in the PowerPoint window where you create the presentation, and which contains three areas, the Slide pane, the Outline tab, Slides tab, and the Notes pane.

Preserve a master Feature that keeps a slide master from being deleted if no slides use it in the presentation. A pushpin icon next to a master indicates it is preserved.

Preview Shows how your slides will print using the current print settings before you actually print them.

Profile A group of email accounts and address books assigned to a single user in Microsoft Outlook.

Publish a presentation Saving a PowerPoint file as a Web page in html format and placing it on a Web server in order to make your presentation available to users on the Internet.

Rehearse timings Feature that lets you view and then set the timings for the amount of time each slide will appear on screen during a slide show that runs automatically.

Review Accept or reject the collective edits and comments of your colleagues after they have reviewed a presentation.

Review cycle The process of routing a file to a specified group of people, and where all reviewer comments and changes are added to the file along with information about each review pass.

Rich Text Format (RTF) files A file format that can easily be imported or transferred between other application formats. PowerPoint files saved as RTF retain text formatting such as font type and font style but lose any graphics or media files that were part of the original file.

Row label The first column of a table, used to identify the content of each row.

ScreenTip A yellow box containing helpful identifying information that appears when you position the pointer over a toolbar button, a design template on the task pane, and in various other places in the program.

Send To Mail Recipient (as Attachment) Command that emails a PowerPoint file to a designated recipient so that the recipient can open, view, and edit it.

Send To Mail Recipient for Review Command that sends a file to an email recipient and automatically includes a message that requests the recipient to review the attachment.

Send To Routing Recipient Command that sends a PowerPoint the file to more than one reviewer, and lets you specify routing recipients in Add Routing Slip dialog box.

Show popup menu Menu that provides navigation commands and other tools to help you as the slide show is running.

Slide master The part of the presentation that specifies how text and graphics appear on each slide. The slide master stores information about the design template, including placeholder sizes, position, background design, and color schemes.

Slide master pair Consists of a slide master and title master in a presentation.

Slide pane In Normal view, the area where you can see and work on the design and text of a slide.

Slide timings The amount of time each slide appears on the screen in a slide show that is set to run automatically. You can specify the same or different timings for each or all the slides in the show.

Slides tab In Normal view, the tab that shows thumbnails of the slides.

Sound file Any file that contains sound such as music, a speech, or a sound effect such as a train whistle, rocket noise, or bells. Most sound files have a .wav or an .mp3 file extension.

Source file The originating file where a linked or an embedded object was created.

Status bar Area at the bottom of the program window that tells you the slide you are viewing, the total number of slides in the presentation, and the design template used in the presentation. The right side of the status bar has several indicators that appear as you create the presentation to help your work.

Subordinate shape Items at a lower hierarchical level in an organization chart, which are connected by lines to superior shapes in the hierarchy.

Summary slide A slide that includes all the titles from selected slides as a bulleted list to provide your audience with an overview of key points in your presentation.

Superior shapes Items at a higher hierarchical level in an organization chart, which are connected by lines to subordinate shapes in the hierarchy.

Table A structure that organizes data in columns and rows.

Title bar Bar that appears at the top of the program window that has displays the Program name as well as the current filename on the left. On the right are three control buttons for controlling the PowerPoint program window: the Minimize button, the Restore button, and the Close button

Title master The part of the slide master that contains the layout and formatting specifications for the title slide in a presentation.

Toolbar Bar that contains buttons that you can click to access common PowerPoint commands.

Transitions Specified display effects for how one slide leaves the screen and a new slide appears.

Values Data represented along the vertical or Y-axis of a chart.

Video files Files that show motion and could be used to make your points stronger in a variety of ways. Video formats include avi, QuickTime, and mpeg.

View buttons Buttons located below the Slides tab that let you quickly switch between the three main views; **Normal, Slide Sorter,** and **Slide Show.**

Web Archive One file that contains all the files required to display Web pages. Web archives can be sent via email and are more easily transported between computers than htm files.

Word 2002 Word processing software program that is part of the Microsoft Office XP suite of programs.

WordArt A text object with highly stylized effects.

X-axis The horizontal axis of a chart, categories of data from the datasheet.

Y-axis The vertical axis of a chart that contains values of data from the datasheet.

Index